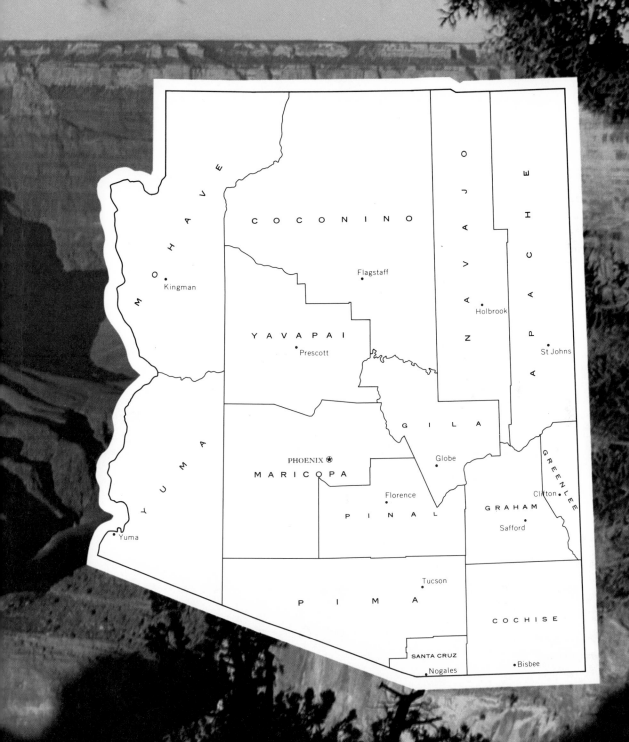

The New

Enchantment of America

ARIZONA

By Allan Carpenter

CHILDRENS PRESS, CHICAGO

ACKNOWLEDGMENTS

For assistance in the preparation of the revised edition, the author thanks:
KEN McCLURE, Director, News Bureau, Arizona Office of Tourism, USDI, EROS Space Project, and USDI, National Park Service.

American Airlines—Anne Vitaliano, Director of Public Relations; *Capitol Historical Society,* Washington, D.C.; *Newberry Library,* Chicago, Dr. Lawrence Towner, Director; *Northwestern University Library,* Evanston, Illinois; *United Airlines*—John P. Grember, Manager of Special Promotions; Joseph P. Hopkins, Manager, News Bureau; Carl Provorse, *Carpenter Publishing House.*

UNITED STATES GOVERNMENT AGENCIES: *Department of Agriculture*—Robert Hailstock, Jr., Photography Division, Office of Communication; Donald C. Schuhart, Information Division, Soil Conservation Service. *Army*—Doran Topolosky, Public Affairs Office, Chief of Engineers, Corps of Engineers. *Department of Interior*—Louis Churchville, Director of Communications; EROS Space Program—Phillis Wiepking, Community Affairs; Charles Withington, Geologist; Mrs. Ruth Herbert, Information Specialist; Bureau of Reclamation; National Park Service—Fred Bell and the individual sites; Fish and Wildlife Service—Bob Hines, Public Affairs Office. *Library of Congress*—Dr. Alan Fern, Director of the Department of Research; Sara Wallace, Director of Publications; Dr. Walter W. Ristow, Chief, Geography and Map Division; Herbert Sandborn, Exhibits Officer. *National Archives*—Dr. James B. Rhoads, Archivist of the United States; Albert Meisel, Assistant Archivist for Educational Programs; David Eggenberger, Publications Director; Bill Leary, Still Picture Reference; James Moore, Audio-Visual Archives. *United States Postal Service*—Herb Harris, Stamps Division.

For assistance in the preparation of the first edition, the author thanks:
Bert Fireman, Executive Vice-President, Arizona Historical Foundation; Sarah Folsom, State Superintendent of Public Instruction; Arizona Development Board; Samuel P. Goddard, Jr., former governor.

Illustrations on the preceding pages:
Cover photograph: View of Tsegi Canyon, USDI, NPS, Navajo National Monument
Page 1: Commemorative stamps of historic interest
Pages 2-3: Evening at Grand Canyon, from Mohave Point.
Page 3: (Map) USDI Geological Survey
Pages 4-5: Phoenix area, EROS Space Photo, USDI Geological Survey, EROS Data Center

Project Editor, Revised Edition:
 Joan Downing
Assistant Editor, Revised Edition:
 Mary Reidy

Library of Congress Cataloging in Publication Data

Carpetner, John Allan, 1917-
 Arizona.

 (His The new enchantment of America)
 SUMMARY: Introduces the Grand Canyon state, its history, famous citizens, and places of interest.
 1. Arizona—Juvenile literature.
[1. Arizona] I. Title. II. Series.
F811.3.C29   979.1   79-11803
ISBN 0-516-04103-7

Contents

A True Story to Set the Scene

A DEPOSED PRINCE OF IMPOSTERS

A printer from Florence named Bill was searching through some old documents in the capitol building at Phoenix in 1893. Suddenly he became very excited. This was what he had been looking for, this might very well bring aid to thousands of people in Arizona who were about to have their property taken away.

Bill was right; his discoveries helped bring to a well-deserved end one of the most brazen careers of fraud in American history. Involved were the rights to eleven million of the choicest acres (almost five million hectares) in Arizona, including the entire Phoenix region. The story of how this fraud was stopped is one of the best examples of the triumph of justice. Because those who were right persisted to the end, it is also one of the most gratifying stories of the enchantment of Arizona.

It all began when a former mule skinner, Confederate private, and horse-car operator, James Addison Reavis, became acquainted with Dr. George M. Willing, Jr. Dr. Willing said he was the heir of Miguel Peralta, who owned a vast land grant in Arizona and New Mexico. Dr. Willing conveniently died (some said he was poisoned), and Reavis claimed that he had been willed the Peralta land title.

Reavis spent several years traveling through Mexico and Arizona, tampering with public records to support his claim. At length he took the title Baron of Arizona and petitioned the United States government to give him the deed to a stretch of land 225 miles (362 kilometers) long and 75 miles (121 kilometers) wide, an area larger than Delaware and Connecticut combined, including Phoenix in the west and extending nearly to Silver City, New Mexico, in the east. At the end of the Mexican War, the government had agreed to honor all legitimate land grants made in the area by the former governments of Spain and Mexico.

Opposite: If Reavis, the swindler, had not been caught, his heirs might have owned downtown Phoenix.

Reavis's title appeared genuine to such experts as lawyer Robert Ingersoll and banker John W. Mackay. There was great consternation in the area. Almost forty thousand people would lose their landholdings. Many of them had toiled a lifetime, fighting off drought and Indians and killing rattlesnakes to maintain their property.

Many landholders paid Reavis what he asked in order to obtain quit claim deeds to their land. Even the Southern Pacific Railroad is said to have paid him $50,000 to guarantee legal claim to use its right of way.

In order to provide even better title to his claim, Reavis found a girl he declared was the Peralta heir and married her. They lived in great style, setting up luxurious homes in Arizona, St. Louis, Washington, and Chihuahua, Mexico. They traveled a great deal and even maintained a sumptuous establishment with a large staff of servants in Madrid. Their children were dressed in purple velvet in keeping with the style of the Baron and Baroness of Arizona.

Reavis proposed to launch big business enterprises and hoped to sell stock—mining ventures, lumber companies, and Peralta Grant development companies. He even planned to dam the Gila River for power and irrigation, twenty years before Theodore Roosevelt Dam was built on the neighboring Salt River for the same purpose.

Then Bill (no last name is known) made his discovery. One Reavis document dated 1748 was printed with type that did not come into use until 1875. Another, dated 1787, was printed on paper with the watermark of a Wisconsin mill founded in 1866. Bill took his findings to his boss, Tom Weedin, publisher of the *Arizona Weekly Enterprise.* Weedin had long asserted the Baron was a phony, and he lost no time in exposing him.

At the trial the entire story came out. The whole thing had been a gigantic fraud perpetrated by Reavis, who has been called "one of the most original and capable minds this generation has produced." A very competent forger, Reavis had spent years altering old Spanish and Mexican documents and creating forged evidence, which he cleverly managed to plant among old documents in Mexican and Spanish libraries and claims offices.

There never had been a Don Miguel de Peralta to whom the king of Spain had given a vast grant. Even Reavis's wife was not who he claimed her to be. Reavis had found a poor Mexican girl in California and convinced her that she was the Peraltas's heir. He had spent years teaching her manners and coaching her about her "wealthy family."

Government agents accumulated a fantastic amount of evidence showing the brilliant forgeries and substitutions Reavis had made in documents all over the world. Of course, the courts denied his claims and he was sent to federal prison for fraud. His disillusioned wife divorced him. After he was released from jail he tried many new schemes, but none of them succeeded, and death came almost unnoticed to the once mighty "Baron of Arizona."

Symphony Hall in Phoenix might have been known as "Reavis Hall."

Lay of the Land

THE GRAND CANYON

A part of Arizona belongs to the entire world in a way that is distinctive from any other single area on earth. This region is considered by some authorities to be the most outstanding natural marvel of all. Noted geologist Clarence E. Dutton called it "by far the most sublime of all earthly spectacles." Explorer John W. Powell said that from it "a concept of sublimity can be obtained never again to be equalled on the hither side of paradise." Others have declared that it has an "awful immensity" and "overwhelming boldness."

They were referring to the greatest of all the many wonders that dot the land of Arizona—the Grand Canyon of the Colorado River.

Parts of the Grand Canyon that can be seen today are almost as old as the earth itself. Their age is estimated at a billion and a half years. The canyon itself is young as time is measured in geology, only about seven million years old. Before the canyon existed, the ancestral Colorado River flowed in about the same course as it does today. When the land began to rise, the river flowed more swiftly. The river was able to cut downward about as swiftly as the land rose, creating a narrow slot in the landscape that grew ever deeper.

The canyon's great width is due to the continuing work of many forces—landslides, chipping away of the rocks by ice and frosts, runoff of water down the sides, the grinding force of sand borne by the wind. All have made the Grand Canyon the world's most spectacular example of erosion. The sand, boulders, and other objects carried along in the swift water helped the river constantly scour and carve deeper into its ancient bed.

The canyon ranges in width from 4 to 14 miles (6.4 to 22.5 kilometers), stretches for an incredible 217 miles (349 kilometers) in length, and is 1 mile (1.6 kilometers) deep on the average. In the various layers of the canyon walls, almost the entire history of the

Opposite: The Grand Canyon has been described as "one of the noblest expressions of world geology and geography."

13

Sedona lies in a valley.

formation of the earth, beginning with the original granite of the planet's crust, can be described. Many of the geological periods of millions of years are represented by the various colors: the lavender-brown Tapeats sandstone, the broad green of Cambrian time, a pale purple of the Devonian period, the vermillion of the Redwall and brighter reds above it, buff-colored Coconino sandstone, and creamy or gray Kaibab limestone. The mighty forces of the Colorado River have laid them all bare for study.

The various layers of these walls contain the visible remains of living creatures that were buried there in ancient times. These begin with one-celled plants called algae, going through layers of trilobites (ancient crabs), seaweeds, shells, fossil fish, shark teeth, corals, fern prints, tracks of primitive four-footed animals, sponges, amphibians, reptiles, and other animals.

THE REGIONS OF ARIZONA

Magnificent as it is, the Grand Canyon covers only a small part of Arizona. A land of great variety with almost every type of topography, Arizona contains many other wonders, many almost as grand in their way as the Grand Canyon.

With an area of nearly 114,000 square miles (295,000 square kilometers), Arizona ranks sixth in size of all the states. One tired pioneer crossing the weary miles exclaimed, "I can't see what God Almighty made so much land for!" But today there hardly can be enough of such a country.

Arizona is divided into three major geographical regions: the high, dry plateau country of the north and northeast; the mountain and valley country that sweeps in a lofty diagonal arc from northwest to southeast; and the plains section, including the flat, dry desert floor, in the southwest.

The entire state slopes gradually to the southwest, away from the Continental Divide.

Sand verbenas bloom in spring on the desert.

"SUPPORTERS OF THE SKY"

The land of Arizona ranges from a low point of 137 feet (42 meters) above sea level near Yuma to the 12,670-foot (3,862-meter) height of Humphreys Peak in the San Francisco Peaks. These mountains were called "supporters of the sky" by the Navajo, who thought they were so high that the sun shone on one side at the same time as the moon shone on the other.

The White Mountains, the Santa Catalina Mountains, and the mysterious Chiricahuas are other well-known ranges of the state.

There are thirty separate mountain chains of the basin and range type. Even the plains section is punctuated at intervals by low and handsome purple-looking mountains, some as high as 6,000 feet (1,829 meters).

WATERS IN A THIRSTY LAND

In addition to the Colorado River, the Gila and Little Colorado are two Arizona rivers included in the United States Geological Survey list of principal rivers of the United States. The Bill Williams River is another principal tributary of the Colorado, which drains most of the state.

The most important tributary of the Gila is the Salt River. The Salt, Little Colorado, and San Francisco all have their sources on the slopes of Mount Baldy in the White Mountains.

In contrast with the Colorado, which runs continuously and carries huge flows as rapidly as twenty miles (thirty-two kilometers) an hour, many Arizona streams flow only after rains. One of these is the Agua Fria River; its flow ranges from zero to 100,000 cubic feet (2,832 cubic meters) per second, depending on the volume of rainfall. The Santa Cruz and San Pedro rivers are others that flow only during rainy periods.

The Hassayampa River has an interesting reputation. Drinking its waters is said to produce strange effects. Legend has it that anyone who drinks from certain portions of the river will never tell the truth thereafter. In Arizona during pioneer days, calling a person a Hassayamp was calling him a scamp.

There are sixty-nine lakes in Arizona, the majority of them artificial, as are all the largest lakes. The biggest lakes are shared with neighbors: Lake Mead with Nevada, Lake Powell with Utah, and Havasu Lake with California. The greater part of Lake Powell is in Utah. Roosevelt Lake and San Carlos Lake are also artificial.

Altogether there are 334 square miles (865 square kilometers) of inland water in Arizona.

IN ANCIENT TIMES

The most striking fact about ancient times in what is now such a dry land is that much of present-day Arizona was covered by shallow seas—not once, but many times and in several different areas—to greater and lesser extents.

During the Devonian period, the sea floor was carpeted with a type of clam. So many of these grew, died, and left their shells that today the people of Arizona constuct their buildings and plaster their houses with the limestone formed when these ancient shells were compressed into rock over eons of time.

During this same period the first animals are thought to have emerged from these ancient seas to the land, and their tracks may still be seen in some aged stones. Then the land slowly rose, and the seas went southward. No one knows exactly how many times this rising and submerging occurred. At one time much of Arizona was muddy swamp, where prehistoric dinosaurs and amphibians splashed and gamboled. Their tracks and marks are visible in the ancient mud—now hardened into rock.

After the period of reptiles, seas again covered much of Arizona, even into the northern parts. The land lifted again in what is called the Eocene period. Almost at once, water and wind began eroding the surface to form canyons, mesas, and buttes. Another uplift of land still further changed the surface. Then, from beneath the earth violent volcanic eruptions tossed mountains skyward.

Volcanic activity continued in three periods over a very long time, creating among other natural features the lofty San Francisco Peaks. There are two hundred extinct volcanoes in the Flagstaff area alone. Some authorities feel that volcanic activity was still continuing in what is now Arizona when the early Spaniards came into the region. Sunset Crater was formed as recently as 1064 A.D.

Throughout much of Arizona the history of the earth can be read in the rocks, where the remains of ancient plants and animals continue to tell about their life. Possibly the most spectacular remains are those of once great forests. The trees were covered with silt thousands of feet deep brought in by rivers. Minerals from this silt seeped into the pores of the trees and gradually turned them to stone. In modern times the dirt covering was washed away from some of these, leaving what is probably the world's finest petrified forest—Petrified Forest National Park, in east-central Arizona.

One of the first explorers to write about this area was A.W. Whipple, who in 1853 wrote that he had found a place "where trees have been converted into jaspar." The Indians have a legend that a goddess came into the region, tired and hungry. She killed a rabbit and tried to cook it using wood from the trees. Because it was too green to burn, she became so angry that she turned all the trees to stone so that no one else could ever use them for fuel.

Today the land lies much as the tremendous forces of nature have left it over the past several thousand years. Changes continue, although at a snail's pace as man calculates time. Rocky spires and formations, curiously shaped valleys cleft deeply into the ground, caves, waterfalls, and silent and mysterious expanses of sand and rocks combine to make the surface of Arizona one of the most interesting places in all the world.

CLIMATE

During daylight hours in Arizona, the sun shines more than 80 percent of the time. Arizona residents boast that the air is so clear that cowboys can see a girl wink a mile away. The combination

Petrified Forest.

of sunshine, low humidity, and crystal-clear air became one of the state's greatest natural resources.

Because of the differences in elevation, Arizona has weather for everyone's taste at almost any time of the year. During the winter the lower regions are warm, and the highlands offer winter sports. In summer the lower regions are very hot but dry and almost universally air conditioned, and mountain regions are cool and inviting.

Rainfall varies from less than three inches (about eight centimeters) per year in some areas to thirty inches (seventy-six centimeters) in mountain locations. Rainfall is heaviest in the periods December to February and July and August. The state average of precipitation is 13.69 inches (34.77 centimeters) per year. When rain does come it comes quickly, sweeping across vast areas in a path that can be followed easily by the eye. The line between a rainstorm and dry weather is so marked that jokesters insist a man can wash his hands in an Arizona thunderstorm without wetting his cuffs.

19

Footsteps on the Land

VILLAGES OF THE PAST

Human beings lived in what is now Arizona at least twenty thousand years ago and probably much earlier. This early but quite well-developed civilization is known as Cochise Man. Scanty traces are still found that show these people killed mastodons and practiced agriculture in the Sulphur Spring Valley of southeastern Arizona.

Much later, inhabitants known as the Basketmakers—because of their ability to weave articles, particularly round, coiled baskets—inhabited the area. When these early people left their cave homes, they began to make dwellings called pit houses. The lower parts were pits dug in the ground, with the aboveground components formed from thin slabs of stone.

The early Basketmakers did not know of the bow and arrow but used a sling called the *atlatl* for throwing spears. They grew squash and maize. As the years went by, they learned the use of bows and arrows, the cultivation of beans, and the making of pottery. Gradually the Basketmakers left their pit houses and began living in rectangular houses of stone masonry above the ground.

Later occupants of northern and eastern Arizona came to be known as Pueblo people. Pueblo is a Spanish word meaning village, so these were simply people of the villages. It is not known whether this civilization was a later development of the Basketmakers or whether outsiders came in and destroyed or absorbed the Basketmakers in a new and more advanced civilization.

The Pueblo period in Arizona dates from about 700 A.D through the late 1200s.

As time went on, the Pueblo built larger and larger houses. Some, made of adobe or stone, were known as clan houses. They were built in an L-shape or U-shape, only one story high. Others had as many as fourteen rooms.

Later, during the Great Pueblo period, grand apartment houses

Opposite: The Watch Tower at Desert View is a replica of the lookouts built by prehistoric dwellers.

Some puebloes are open to visitors.

were built with as many as four stories and dozens of rooms. The villages or pueblos, which have been preserved to a surprising degree in the dry Arizona air, are among the most extraordinary treasures of the state. These fantastic structures are found in many parts of Arizona.

For protection, many pueblos were built high up in open-faced caves or great slits in canyon walls. Some of the pueblos were so lofty it seems impossible that they could serve as dwellings. Steps were carved in the stone walls to a certain point, then ladders were used; these were drawn up after the people had entered the pueblo. Some of the best preserved of these cliff pueblos are found in Canyon de Chelly National Monument, where there are 300 prehistoric sites and 138 major ruins. Remains of almost all the prehistoric cultures of the Southwest are found here.

The most spectacular dwelling is the White House, taking its name from a long wall covered with white plaster. It perches in a mouthlike opening of the cliff, and from a distance looks like some great European castle. Mummy Cave Ruin in Canyon del Muerto (Canyon of the Dead) includes a surprising three-story tower house.

Ruins in Montezuma Castle National Monument near Camp Verde are so well preserved that even the ceiling timbers are intact in many rooms. This pinkish-colored castle looms in a recess at the midpoint of a 150-foot (46-meter) vertical cliff. A series of ladders placed against the cliff permitted residents to reach their aerie. The finger marks of the early masons can still be seen in some of the adobe bricks.

More than eight hundred prehistoric home sites are found at Wupatki National Monument. Walnut Canyon National Monument contains more than three hundred dwellings. A hilltop pueblo of a hundred rooms is the main feature of Tuzigoot National Monument.

Montezuma Castle National Monument.

Winter snows sometimes cover Wupatki Ruin and the deserts of Northern Arizona.

In 1064 A.D. a volcano erupted north of the present site of Flagstaff. This is now called Sunset Crater National Monument. The date of the eruption has been determined by examination of the timbers taken from homes that were covered by the volcanic ash. The volcanic ash made the region more fertile, and after a time fairly large numbers of people came in to farm, particularly in what is now Wupatki National Monument. Among the most interesting relics at Wupatki are an open-air amphitheater and a ball court. Nothing is known of the performances that were given in the amphitheater or the games played in the ball court.

In many of these ruins across the state archeologists have found interesting items made and used by Pueblo people—much jewelry, including turquoise pieces such as ear pendants, rings, and necklaces; jugs; clay effigies, ollas, and ladles; woven-basket arm bands still circling arm bones; and many other things. At Kinishba, near White River, an underground ceremonial chamber provided one of the greatest treasures of ancient times ever found, including over a thousand gypsum pendants and an ancient soapstone jewelry piece, evidently designed to be worn in the lips as earrings are worn in the ears.

The Pueblo people were farmers, growing corn, beans, pumpkins, sunflowers, and even cotton, which they learned to weave into cloth. Common plants were used for food, dye, fiber, medicine, fuel, and some construction. Coiled black pottery was common, and a type of pottery known as corrugated ware was also produced. The various tribes traded items quite extensively.

In the late 1200s droughts came and continued for many years. Eventually, the Pueblo people were forced to leave their pueblos and find homes elsewhere, probably farther south.

HOHOKAM—THE ANCIENT ONES

During much of the time the Pueblo inhabited the plateau country, another group of prehistoric people was developing in the desert regions. The Pima Indians refer to these people as the Hohokam, meaning "the ancient ones."

Hohokam people were sometimes known as the Canal Builders because they were competent engineers of irrigation systems. Much of the present-day irrigation system in the Phoenix region follows the Hohokam canal pattern.

Pueblo Grande and Casa Grande stand as remnants of the Hohokam culture. Casa Grande Tower in Casa Grande National Monument has been called "America's first skyscraper." In it, prehistoric architecture in the United States probably reached its greatest achievement. It is thought that when the Pueblo people left their homes, some of them came into the region and taught many of their architectural skills to the Hohokam. The walls of the tower rise about forty feet (twelve meters) above the desert floor, and the central part of the tower is four stories tall.

Many people have puzzled over the "calendar holes" there. The rising sun shines through one of these holes and almost strikes a hole on the opposite wall. This happens only on March 7 and October 7. Before the walls settled, the sun's rays may have struck the other hole precisely on those days, and this may have been the Hohokam way of telling time.

A seashell decorated with a square and compass emblem found at Casa Grande provides another puzzle, since these objects were not supposed to be known there. Some of the turquoise inlaid jewelry found at Casa Grande is among the finest found in any American ruin. Experts are also surprised at the handwoven cloth of very fine grade with its punch-work embroidery.

Hohokam relics are continually being turned up in the Phoenix area. Other prehistoric artifacts of varying periods and peoples are found in many parts of the state. Many picture writings or pictographs can still be seen. Some were made in very ancient times and others by Indians in the historic periods. A good example of the latter is the work in Hieroglyph Canyon in Phoenix South Mountain Park and at Painted Rocks State Historical Site, near Gila Bend.

PEACEFUL AND NOT SO PEACEFUL—THE INDIANS

When Europeans first came into the region that is now Arizona, they found three great language groups of Indians living there: Athapascan, Yuman, and Uto-Aztecan. The Uto-Aztecan included the Kaibab Paiute, Pima and Papago, and Hopi. Experts think that the Hopi were the only Indians remaining in Arizona who could trace their ancestry back to the Pueblo Indians. The first Europeans found them living in pueblos; raising squash, corn, and beans; and grinding corn into fine meal from which a thin bread, piki, was made. The Hopi made fine-quality baskets and pottery, and lived a measured life of ceremonials that included dancing and prayer for health, rain, good fortune, and other favors of their gods. This tribe was a matriarchal people (women ruled), and property was inherited through the female line. The Hopi have changed their everyday life patterns very little in four centuries—as a tribe, probably less than any other aboriginal group in the nation.

The Pima Indians are the "river dwellers" of southern Arizona. They were noted for their generosity to travelers. One traveler wrote: "To us it was a rare sight to be thrown in the midst of a large nation of what are termed wild Indians surpassing many of the Christian nations in agriculture, little behind them in the useful arts, and immeasurably before them in honesty and virtue. During the whole of yesterday our camp was full of men, women and children, who wandered among our packs unwatched and not a single instance of theft was reported."

The Pima and Papago (meaning "bean people") considered themselves one family. They made unusual use of the desert's poor offerings. Yucca provided thread and materials for sandals and baskets; the yucca fruit was eaten. The first day of the native year was considered the day the saguaro cactus ripened, usually in late May or June. They ate some of the fruit fresh, pressed and dried some in cake form, and boiled the juice for syrup. They ground the black seeds into chicken feed. The fibers were used for building, and the knots, formed where woodpeckers bored into the trunk, were used for drinking cups.

When the first settlers came into the region later, the Papago became noted as their constant and faithful friends.

The Athapascan family had only two tribes in Arizona, but these constituted the largest number of Indians in the region. They were the Navajo and Apache, who both arrived in the area shortly before the first Europeans. Navajo now are thought to have entered about five hundred years ago. In the early times of exploration in the region, the Navajo and Apache were considered almost identical, but they grew more different over the years. The word Navajo is thought to come from the word *navaju,* meaning cultivated land in a canyon. The word *navajo* is also the Spanish word for knife.

"Capturing wild horses" by George Catlin.

At first the Navajo were a rather insignificant tribe, but grew stronger by stealing sheep and horses that had been left among the Pueblo tribes by early Spaniards. Instead of eating the sheep at once as most tribes did, they carefully tended them and increased the flocks. As a pastoral people, their wealth and power increased. They continually preyed on the Pueblo people and later on the Spanish settlements in the entire Southwest.

The Apache were a fierce yet religious people. Their deity, known as Usen, could be approached only indirectly through the sun, moon, or lightning or through snakes, owls, and other creatures. The Apache were very close to animals, considering birds their next of kin and the animals their little brothers. They considered that during hibernation the bear communicated with the spirit world and brought back its new knowledge to the medicine men. Legal ownership of tribal property belonged to the women. Men became members of their wife's group upon marriage, and children were considered property of the mother. In each tribal group there was a male chief of war, but other matters were ruled by a female chief.

The Yuman family had many smaller Indian groups in what is now Arizona. One of the smallest but most interesting was the Havasupai. They probably never numbered more than two or three

28

hundred people. When Europeans first met the Havasupai, they were living in the awesome isolation of Cataract Canyon in the very bottom of the Grand Canyon. They still make their home there today, living in about the same way as in earlier times.

Closely related to the Havasupai are the Hualpai, the "pine tree folk." The Mojave were once the most warlike of all the Yuman tribes. They delighted in hand-to-hand combat with clubs and when outnumbered generally fought to the death.

Yavapai, Cocopah, Yuma, Maricopa, and Chemehuevis are other Indian groups that inhabited the area when the early settlers came to what is now Arizona.

SEVEN CITIES AND SAINTLY SERVICE

There may have been Europeans in what is now Arizona as early as 1526. Some accounts say that Jose de Basconales, an officer of Cortes, the conqueror of Mexico, reached Arizona in that year, but whether he came that far north is now considered unlikely. Alvar Nunez Cabeza de Vaca and three companions, Castillo and Dorantes and their black slave, Estevan, in 1536 made an incredible trip across country from the Gulf of Mexico, where they had been captives of the Indians. It is possible that they crossed part of what is now Arizona in their tortured wanderings, but their exact route has not been established.

It is known, however, that a Franciscan friar, Marcos de Niza, accompanied by Estevan, who had been freed, explored part of Arizona in 1539. They had been sent by the viceroy of New Spain to find the fabled Seven Cities of Cibola. These cities were supposedly places of great wealth with streets paved in gold and castles decorated with precious jewels.

A Father Onorato started the journey with them but became ill and was left behind at an Indian village in northern Mexico. Father de Niza continued without him, sending Estevan on ahead. Estevan crossed the Pima Indian country wearing a costume of brilliant feathers and tinkling bells. The superstitious Pima were awed by his appearance and let him pass, but when he reached the Pueblo city of Hawikuh (near present-day Gallup, New Mexico), the Zuni Indians executed him. Father de Niza heard of Estevan's death while still some distance from his goal.

At a distance, Hawikuh seemed as magnificent as legend had reported. Fearing to go closer, Father de Niza returned to Mexico and gave a glowing but exaggerated report of what he had found.

In 1540, the next year, hoping to gain the Indian riches to the north, the Spanish sent a great expedition under Francisco Vásquez de Coronado, with Father de Niza as guide. The impressive company followed the San Pedro River to the Gila and then traveled northeast, leaving what is now Arizona. They finally found the squalid stone villages, and Coronado was greatly disappointed by their lack of wealth.

A much more important discovery was made by an assistant of Coronado, Garcia Lopez de Cardenas. Hearing from the Indians of a great river to the northwest, Coronado sent Cardenas and a party of twelve men to find it. After traveling twenty days, the expedition reached the brink of a great gorge. What looked like a small river flowed ribbonlike at the bottom of the chasm.

Although the Indians advised against it, the men tried to climb to the bottom. However, they reported that the buttes and spires that "appeared from above to be the height of a man were higher than the tower of the Cathedral of Seville." They gave up the climb. They had, of course, discovered the Grand Canyon of the Colorado River.

To early explorers, the canyon was simply an awesome obstacle keeping them away from the life-giving waters of the river flowing through what seemed to them only immense desolation. Even much later, James O. Pattie described the "horrid mountains which cage it up, as to deprive all human beings of the ability to descend its banks and make use of its water." Joseph Ives said in 1857, "ours has been the first and will doubtless be the last party of whites to visit this profitless locality." He was an even lesser prophet than he was a historian.

At about the same time Coronado's men were trying to reach the waters of the Colorado River to the north, Hernando de Alarcon boldly reached the mouth of the Colorado River and poled and rowed laboriously north, the first European to sail on the Colorado River. He went up the river as far as present-day Yuma, Arizona, attempting to locate and supply Coronado's land expedition.

When Coronado returned in disgrace to report that there appeared to be no great wealth to the north, Spain abandoned its interest in the region for forty years.

In 1580, Father Agustin Rodriguez and another priest came north into New Mexico with an escort of soldiers to do missionary work among the Indians. When the soldiers found rich silver ore near the Gila River, they deserted the priests. The next year Antonio de Espejo was sent with a small expedition to rescue the priests. He found that they had been killed by the Indians, but he continued westward in what might be called the first mineral prospecting trip in Arizona history. Near the forks of the Bill Williams River west of Prescott, he found rich silver ore deposits.

Although Espejo returned to report his discovery of the wealth sought by the rulers of New Spain, no further attempt to enter the northern region was made until sixteen years later. Then Juan de Oñate brought several hundred people from Mexico City into New Mexico as colonists and formally claimed for Spain the great region of New Mexico, including Arizona. In later expeditions, de Oñate apparently rediscovered the silver source found by Espejo, but the Spaniards did not mine this wealth.

MEN WITH A MISSION

One of many mysterious Indian legends is the story of the strange lady in blue. When Christian missionaries first came into the Arizona region, they found that some of the Indians had already adopted the precepts of Christianity. They said their ancestors had been taught the Christian religion by a beautiful lady dressed in blue. Strangely, a very devout lady of Spain, Marie Coronel de Agreda, head of an order that wore blue robes, said that she had made many visits to the New World and described many tribes not yet seen by the explorers. However, Marie Agreda was never known to have left Spain, and so the mystery stands.

It is known, however, that Franciscan priests began missionary work among the Hopi Indians in the early 1600s. They baptized converts and built chapels in the midst of the Hopi pueblos.

In 1680, the priests were killed and the churches burned in an Indian uprising. From that time on, the Hopi took little or no interest in the Europeans' religion.

In 1692 the Jesuit order began work among the Indians in northern Mexico and southern Arizona, a district they called Pimeria Alta. The most noted Jesuit missionary in Pimeria Alta was Father Eusebio Francisco Kino, whose work is discussed in more detail in a later section.

Father Kino's many accomplishments included the arduous task of establishing twenty-four missions in Pimeria Alta. Seven missions were located in what is now Arizona. One of these was Tumacacori, near Nogales, the ruins of which are now a national monument. Another for which Father Kino laid the foundation was the famed San Xavier del Bac mission, the northern outpost of the mission chain known as the White Dove of the Desert, near Tucson.

This beautiful building (finished in 1798), called by some the finest Spanish mission in the United States, was built by unskilled Indians. To construct the dome, engineers working under the direction of the padres filled the church with dirt, piling it into a mold in the desired shape for the dome. Then the dome masonry was built around the earth mold. When the dome was finished, according to unconfirmed legend, the priests told the Indians they had scattered gold coins through the dirt. The dirt was quickly carried out and disposed of by eager treasure hunters, leaving the sturdy structure standing much as it does today.

Father Kino visited the ruins of Casa Grande in 1694; in his writings he notes: "The Casa Grande—a four story building as large as a castle and equal to the finest church in these lands of Sonora."

After Father Kino's death in 1711, missionary work declined in Pimeria Alta. There were no forts or Spanish troops stationed in what is now Arizona. The Apache, and in lesser degree the Pima and

White Dove of the Desert.

Papago, committed so many acts of thievery and murder that it became almost impossible for Europeans to stay in the region without protection. In 1752 Tubac, the first presidio, or fort, was established in the Santa Cruz valley. It is the oldest European settlement in what is now Arizona. Tucson was founded in 1776 as a presidio of the Spanish army. In 1767 the Jesuits were removed by the government of New Spain from their missions, and the Franciscans were asked to take over the management of missions and mission work.

The change brought in another of Arizona's remarkable priests— Padre Francisco Tomas Garcés, who made San Xavier del Bac his headquarters. Father Kino had started the original mission more than sixty-five years before. Garcés receives the credit for starting work on the present structure and inspiring its completion. He carried the mission work as far west as the Colorado River, where he began to teach Christianity to the Yuma Indians. When a group of

33

Spanish soldiers pastured their horses in the Yuma's vital bean fields and when some would-be Spanish settlers took over some of the Yuma lands, the Yuma became enraged. Father Garcés was clubbed to death as he said mass, and all the soldiers were killed. The mission was not completed until long after Garcés' death.

The Indian participants in the uprising were punished a year later and a treaty was also made with the Apache, but during the Mexican wars for independence against Spain, the Indians again rose up. Hundreds of settlers were killed. The new Mexican republic took over and established the territory of Nuevo Mexico, including present-day New Mexico and Arizona. The government expelled the Franciscan missionaries in 1827. What is now the state of New Mexico was prosperous, but present-day Arizona had been almost abandoned.

The small towns of Tubac and Tucson, each with a tiny garrison of soldiers for protection, were about all that remained.

UNITED STATES BEGINNINGS

By the 1820s American prospectors and trappers had penetrated the territory of Nuevo Mexico. Typical of these men was the famed and picturesque trapper Bill Williams. In 1846 the United States had declared war on Mexico, and Colonel Stephen W. Kearny had captured Santa Fe, the capital of Nuevo Mexico, without bloodshed. In September of that year, Kearny marched west to help conquer California. He met the most noted of all scouts, Kit Carson, on his way east to report that most of California was in American hands. Carson reversed his direction in order to guide Kearny's army across the wilds of Arizona.

At Carson's suggestion the troops abandoned the heavy wagons, loading their supplies on pack mules. But the going was still difficult. They suffered from hunger and thirst on long stretches of the journey through Arizona. Deep canyons and rugged mountains forced them into many tiring detours.

A second group of soldiers made their weary way across Arizona

34

after Kearny. The renowned Mormon Battalion, consisting of volunteers, had left their fellow Mormons at Council Bluffs, Iowa, and started to California to fight in the war there. By the time they reached their destination the war was over, but they had made the longest infantry march on record.

Some of the most difficult parts of the Mormon route were in Arizona. Approaching Tucson, they were concerned with the number of defenders of the town, but decided to venture through it anyway since it would save them 100 miles (161 kilometers) of travel. One of the men, Henry Standage, reports in his journal for December 16, 1846, that Lieutenant Colonel Philip St. George Cooke, their leader, "determined to pass through. . . . Many of the brethren traveled this 18 miles without either food or drink, suffering much for want of water, having none last night or yesterday.

"When we arrived at the town, we found but a few of the inhabitants, the soldiery having fled with their cannon and also having forced many of the people to leave also. We were kindly treated by the people of Touson [Tucson] who brought flour, meal, tobacco, quinces to the camp for sale and many of them giving such things to the soldiers. We camped about a half mile from the town. The colonel suffered no private property to be touched, neither was it in the heart of any man to my knowledge so to do."

On December 18 they "traveled till 8 in the evening, camped without water after traveling 30 miles. December 19, started again by day light and traveled fast towards the Ela [Gila] River. Traveled till a little after dark and still no prospects of water. . . . I was almost choked with thirst and hardly able to stand when I stopped." Some of the men found a little muddy water standing in holes "and followed on towards the river, passed by many lying on the road side begging for water, not having found the place we did." They finally reached the river, and sent water back to those who had collapsed on the way.

The main accomplishment of the Mormon Battalion was to blaze a wagon train trail from Santa Fe to the West Coast.

When the war with Mexico ended in 1848, the Treaty of Guadalupe Hidalgo provided that the part of Arizona north of the

Gila River would be transferred to the United States. In 1853, United States Minister to Mexico, James Gadsden, arranged for the United States to buy what has been called the Gadsden Purchase, giving Arizona its present southern boundary with Mexico.

Meanwhile, much had been happening. What is now Arizona was made part of the territory of New Mexico in 1850. Swarms of people had migrated across the region, desperately trying to reach the gold of California as quickly as possible. Where only a few Indians and Spaniards had been before, a total of sixty thousand people passed through Arizona. Some, finding pleasant places, decided to go no farther and set up farms or ranches in the territory. Others were buried in lonely graves along the trail or their bones were bleached in the sun after they were killed in Indian attacks or died from thirst or other privations of the hard journey.

One Indian attack came to be known as the Oatman Massacre. On its way to California, the Oatman wagon train was attacked by Yavapai Indians in 1851. The Oatman father and mother and a baby were killed, and the Indians thought a son was dead; they took the two daughters prisoner. The younger sister died in captivity, but the older girl—Olive—lived for many years with Indians until she was ransomed. The son, Lorenzo Oatman, survived and was reunited with his sister.

Transportation improved markedly in the territory. Passengers and freight were carried up the Colorado River from the Gulf of California, unloading at Yuma for points in southern Arizona and stopping at La Paz or Ehrenberg for the central section. By 1857 a stage line was running across the state. Almost as much time was spent out of the stage as in, however, plodding through stretches of shifting sand.

Arizona pioneer Charles D. Poston first came to Arizona in 1854 and soon afterwards organized some of the state's earliest commercial developments. These ventures included silver and copper mining and smelting, and trading. When gold was discovered twenty-five miles (forty kilometers) north of Fort Yuma in 1858, Gila City sprang up with a population of a thousand. The gold quickly gave out, and Gila City became the first of Arizona's many ghost towns.

By that year Arizona's oldest community, Tubac, had a population of eight hundred. Charles Poston later described the community: "We had no law but love, no occupation but labor; no government; no taxes; no public debt; no politics. It was a community in a perfect state of nature. As syndic [a government officer] under New Mexico, I opened a book of records, performed the marriage ceremony, baptized the children and granted the divorce."

CIVIL WAR ON THE FRONTIER

A large percentage of the settlers in Arizona during this period had come from Southern states. It was not surprising, therefore, when Arizona residents held conventions at Tucson and Mesilla in 1861 and voted to make their region a part of Confederate territory. In January 1862, President Jefferson Davis of the Confederate States declared that Arizona was a territory of the Confederacy. A force of Confederate cavalry from Texas arrived at Tucson in February 1862, under the direction of Captain Sherod Hunter. Federal troops from California occupied Yuma and made it their headquarters for a drive eastward to dislodge the Confederates.

Only one important Civil War skirmish occurred on Arizona soil. Captain Hunter had captured Union supplies and nine Union men at the Pima villages. A small group of Union cavalry under Lieutenant James Barrett probed southward to Piccho Peak to attack the Confederate pickets before larger Union supporting forces had arrived. Barrett and two of his men died in the engagement, and three were captured. Confederate losses were lighter, but they withdrew to Tucson and within a few weeks retreated to the Rio Grande.

Until this time, the government at Washington D.C. had taken little interest in distant Arizona. Now, however, the Union needed money to finance the war, and the gold of Arizona began to look attractive. Congress created the territory of Arizona on February 24, 1863. Late in the year (December 29, 1863), John N. Goodwin arrived in Arizona as first governor of the territory, with the temporary capital at Fort Whipple in Little Chino Valley.

Yesterday and Today

RISING FROM ITS ASHES

In the early territorial period, the city of Phoenix had its rather unusual beginnings. John Y.T. Smith had started a hay camp in the area in 1866 to supply fodder to Camp McDowell, an army post about thirty miles (forty-eight kilometers) away. When Jack Swilling passed the hay camp in 1867, he was impressed with the importance of the canals made by the prehistoric Hohokam people. He was among the first to see that with comparatively little effort the old irrigation system could be restored, using water from nearby Salt River.

He persuaded some Wickenburg residents to invest in his Swilling Irrigation Canal Company. Within a short period several of the old canals had been put in operation again, and a number of ranches were created. Before a year had passed, crops were harvested on the ruins of the ancient Hohokam civilization.

An English "adventurer, scholar, and inebriate," Darrel Duppa, visiting the young community, remembered the mythical bird, the Phoenix. At the end of every five hundred year period, as the bird began to grow old, it was burned completely by fire, then rose again young and fresh from its ashes. Seeing a new civilization rising on the ruins of the old one in this area, Duppa suggested that the community be named in honor of the mythical bird, and so the crude and struggling village received its fascinating name—Phoenix.

The first building erected in what is now the city of Phoenix was occupied by Hancock's Store, a combination courthouse, justice's office, store, and butcher shop. About once a week, a cow was butchered and hung in the store. Each customer brought a knife and cut away his own order, at a price of about thirty cents per pound (sixty-six cents per kilogram). More construction soon followed, and before long there was a main street lined with buildings, including the Phoenix Hotel. Modern owners of swimming pools will be

Opposite: Modern travelers find few of the earlier hazards of the trail.

interested to know that the hotel's first bathtub was actually a pool with water supplied by a running canal, thoughtfully covered by a canvas awning. With these small beginnings, the business and resort activities of the future metropolis were on their way.

WARPATH!

Arizona may hold some kind of record for the length and severity of warfare between the settlers and Indians. There were probably more capable and dedicated leaders among the Indians of Arizona than anywhere else. Added to this was the large and militant Indian population that could retreat into almost impenetrable mountain and canyon hideaways. These factors gave Arizona an unmatched history of Indian warfare, from the beginning of European exploration extending almost into the twentieth century.

In July 1862 one of the largest Indian battles in Arizona history took place in Apache Pass, when Union forces marching toward New Mexico met the Apache forces of Chief Cochise and Chief Mangas Coloradas. Although the government men had marched most of the day without water, they stood their ground, brought out their howitzers, and the Indians at last retreated. One of them later said, "We would have done well if you hadn't fired wagon wheels at us."

Cochise had not battled extensively against settlers until he had been arrested and accused of leading a raid on a ranch; when he denied this, his captors accused him of lying. He escaped almost immediately, and from 1861 until 1872 he led his people in bitter warfare, raiding ranches, settlements, stagecoaches, and emigrant trains, with bloody success.

The United States government never subdued this mighty warrior in his stronghold in the Dragoon Mountains. From this location Cochise terrorized all of southeastern Arizona. Peace came largely through the efforts of Tom Jeffords, who operated a stage line. After the Apache had killed twenty-two drivers in less than two years, Jeffords went alone into the Cochise stronghold. There he and Cochise grew to be friends and finally became "blood brothers."

"The Siege of Tubatama," from a diorama at Tumacacori National Monument.

When at last General O.O. Howard was sent to make peace with Cochise, Jeffords persuaded the chief to meet him for a parley. As the talks went on, Cochise asked his blood brother, "Can this man's word be trusted?"

"I don't know," Jeffords answered, "but I believe it can."

Cochise would only agree to the treaty if Jeffords was appointed Indian agent. Although he said this meant great financial sacrifice to him, Jeffords accepted the post as a public service both to his country and his Indian brothers.

Cochise died, undefeated, and was buried in his Dragoon stronghold. On the night of his burial, Jeffords claimed, his Apache tribesmen raced their horses up and down the canyon until dawn so that the hoof marks would erase every trace of the grave's location. Tom Jeffords said he was the only non-Indian who knew just where the chief was buried. He never disclosed the secret during the forty years he lived after Cochise's death. When the Apache of today go into the mountains to gather beyotas (acorns), they are very respectful of Stronghold Canyon, the spirit land of Cochise.

THE LONG WALK

For a century and a half the Navajo to the north battled Spanish and United States travelers and settlers in their lands. Their stronghold was in the great gash of Canyon de Chelly and Canyon del Muerto. In 1864 the famed frontiersman Kit Carson was sent to capture the Navajo. In a report on the effort, General James H. Carleton wrote: "This is the first time any troops, whether when the country belonged to Mexico or since we acquired it, have been able to pass through the Canyon de Chelly, which, for its great depth, its length, its perpendicular walls, and its labyrinthine character, has been regarded by eminent geologists as the most remarkable of any 'fissure' (for such it is held to be) upon the face of the globe.

"It has been the great fortress of the tribe since time out of mind. To this point they fled when pressed by our troops. . . . Many other commanders have made an attempt to go through it, but had to retrace their steps. It was reserved for Colonel Carson to be the first to succeed. . . .

"I beg respectfully to call the serious attention of the government to the destitute condition of the captives, and beg for authority to provide clothing for the women and children. . . . Whatever is done should be done at once. At all events, as I before wrote you, 'we can feed them cheaper than we can fight them.' "

More than eight thousand Navajo were led on what they called the Long Walk to captivity on a reservation in eastern New Mexico. When this reservation proved unsuccessful, the Navajo were permitted to return to their ancestral lands, where they remain today.

GERONIMO!

Some of the last Indian uprisings in the United States were directed by Chief Geronimo. He had early vowed vengeance on all settlers for the killing of his wife and children by Mexicans. Geronimo was so successful in leading his Apache followers on raids into Mexico that he was made a war chief.

On a number of occasions Geronimo and his band made peace with the government and returned to the reservation, but they usually became unhappy over the food rations and the regulations against drinking *tizwin*, a corn brew.

From 1881 to 1886, Geronimo led several escapes from the reservation, hiding in the mountains of Mexico and raiding ranches and settlements in Mexico, New Mexico, and Arizona. He was captured in Mexico by General George Crook, along with Cochise's son, Natches, but again fled to Mexico. After a long chase, Lieutenant Charles B. Gatewood dramatically walked alone and unarmed into Geronimo's camp and persuaded him to surrender, convincing the old Apache that death for all would be the price of further resistance. After temporary imprisonment at Fort Marion, Florida, in Alabama, and many years at Fort Sill, Oklahoma, Geronimo died at Fort Sill in 1909.

LIVING IN PERIL

Arizona frontier life was for the most part peaceful and far removed from violence, but the dangers of Indian attack and outlaw activity long dominated much of the area.

Apache Pass became the death spot of so many immigrants, soldiers, and prospectors that stagecoach drivers hesitated to pass through it during the Cochise period. Triple pay was offered for the run, but few drivers lived to collect their money. The road from Wickenburg to Ehrenberg once was called the Trail of Graves because of the number of travelers who died along its way either from thirst or in attacks by the Mojave. In its first fifteen years of American settlement, the Wickenburg area lost more than four hundred men, women, and children in Indian attacks.

Once during a trial in the log courthouse called Fort Misery, at Prescott, Indians attacked nearby, and the prisoners at the bar rushed out with the prosecuting lawyer and the judge to defend the town. When the Indians were gone so were the prisoners.

During a raid on a sawmill near Fort Crittenden, the Apache captured Mrs. Larcena Pennington Page, speared her through the back, and threw her over a cliff. She dragged herself across the rocky, brushy country for a night and two days before finding help, but eventually she recovered.

Pioneer John Cady told of the time Indians attacked him and two companions and of how he rode to Fort Crittenden for help: "I look back on that desperate ride now with feelings akin to horror. Surrounded with murderous savages, with only a decrepit mule to ride and fourteen miles to go, it seemed impossible that I could get through safely. My companions said goodbye to me as though I were a scaffold victim about to be executed. But get through I did—how I do not know—and the chilling, weird war-calls of the Indians howling at me from the hills as I rode return to my ears even now with extraordinary vividness."

Noted scout John Townsend was a relentless foe of the Indians, who he thought had killed members of his family. With uncanny ability, he would stalk Indians alone at night, and in this way he took fifty scalps. When he was finally caught in an ambush and killed by his Indian enemies, they did not mutilate his body. In tribute to his bravery, they covered the body with a fine blanket, weighted with stones at the corners.

Large numbers of the Indians took no part in bloodshed, and they often suffered just as the settlers did. Several settlers were murdered near Chief Cassadora's camp at Cassadora Mesa. Troops were sent with orders to take no prisoners, and Cassadora and his tribe fled to the hills. Later Cassadora told the commander, Captain J.M. Hamilton, "We were afraid because some bad Indians had killed white men, so we ran away. That was wrong. We cannot fight for we have no arms or ammunition. Our food is gone; we are suffering from hunger; our moccasins are worn out, you can see our tracks on the rocks where our feet left blood. We do not want to die but if we must, we prefer to die by bullets from your soldiers' guns than from hunger. So we have come to your camp asking for peace." Hamilton gave them food, and asked for the order to be reversed on taking no prisoners. The Indians were returned to their homes.

Chief Eskiminizin had once been a powerful warrior, but he settled down to peaceful ways. He remained friendly to the settlers in spite of the massacre of his family, raids on his farm crops, and the loss of his land to the newcomers.

WILD WEST

The West was never wilder than in early Arizona. Outlaws caused almost as much fear and hardship as the Indians. Ranching and mining were difficult occupations, and many a man died with his boots on. The fame of almost forgotten towns such as Weaver rests chiefly in the many deeds of violence supposedly committed there. Even today at the upper end of this ghost town there is a dilapidated boot hill, "where slayer and slain sleep in nameless graves and peaceful anonymity." Much the same scene can be found in many other parts of the state.

One of the strangest series of events came to be known as the Pleasant Valley War. No one is quite sure just how the war got started, but it had to do with a quarrel between the Graham and Tewksbury families. Their struggle became a five-year feud involving almost everyone in the valley. One of the Tewksbury boys, Jim, is supposed to have been such an expert with a gun that he once reached over his shoulder and shot an enemy without turning around. Before it ended, the Pleasant Valley War had claimed nineteen known victims and there likely were many others.

PEACEFUL GROWTH

Gradually, of course, as more settlers came in and business, mining, and ranching increased, law and order came to Arizona.

After the Civil War, many more settlers emigrated from Southern states, fleeing the hard times of the Reconstruction. Considerable Mormon settlement took place in Arizona in the 1870s and 1880s. Littlefield and Fredonia were founded, and the Mormons built a road into Arizona to Lee's Ferry on the Colorado River. Early towns founded by the Mormons included Snowflake, St. Joseph, Show Low, Mesa City, Jonesville (now Lehi), St. David, Eager, and Springerville.

Soon after the first territorial capital had been set up at Fort Whipple, the army post was moved eighteen miles (twenty-nine kilometers) south to Granite Creek. The government followed the army. A log mansion was built for the governor about a mile from the camp. Around this grew the city of Prescott. In 1867 the capital was moved to Tucson. It was returned to Prescott in 1877 and finally ended up in Phoenix in 1889. When the final change was made, the legislature decided to move by rail. To do this the legislators had to go by way of Los Angeles, because there was no direct railroad to Phoenix from Prescott at the time.

Meanwhile, the natural wonders of the region were becoming widely known. In 1869 one-armed Major John Wesley Powell and his men completed the almost impossible boat trip down the Colorado River through the Grand Canyon. Powell described the scene when Bradley, one of the men, was caught alone in a boat in one of the worst rapids: "she goes down almost beyond our sight . . . then she comes up again on a great wave, and down and up, then around behind some great rocks and is lost in the mad white foam below. We stand frozen with fear, for we see no boat." But Bradley made it and so the others followed him in the other boat.

Powell was responsible for many picturesque names of the region, including Dirty Devil Falls and Bright Angel Falls.

In 1882 the first woman settler, Mrs. Edward Ayres, reached the bottom of the Grand Canyon. Soon, tourist facilities were built in the canyon region. The remarkable ruin of Casa Grande was made a national monument in 1889.

THE STATE OF ARIZONA

The Spanish-American War was the first United States conflict in which many Arizona people took part. Troops from Arizona were in the forefront of Theodore Roosevelt's famous Rough Riders in

46

Cuba. Roosevelt himself once came to Arizona for a mountain lion hunt on the Kaibab Plateau. The Theodore Roosevelt Dam on the Salt River, completed in 1911, was the first federal reclamation project, an extremely important factor in the state's growth.

As early as 1892 a bill to create a state of Arizona was introduced in Congress, but it did not pass. Another plan for admitting Arizona and New Mexico as one state was defeated by the people of Arizona. Then in 1912 Congress authorized and President William Howard Taft signed a proclamation making Arizona the forty-eighth state, with a state constitution carefully designed to protect the power and rights of the people.

Mexican revolutionary Pancho Villa captured the Mexican town of Sonora, the twin of Nogales on the Arizona side, in 1916. When he threatened to attack Nogales, Arizona, the border was barricaded and the United States prepared for defense. Ten thousand National Guardsmen arrived. When Villa's soldiers prepared to blow up the barricades, the United States troops opened fire; many of Villa's men were killed and the others retreated to the south. The border was soon reopened.

In 1918 a Mexican smuggler was shot at Nogales by a United States customs guard. Relations between Americans and Mexicans grew more and more strained. In the ensuing conflict, thirty-two Americans, among them Captain Lungerford, and seventy or eighty Mexicans, including the mayor of Mexican Nogales, were killed. An armistice was finally reached between the governors of Arizona and Sonora, Mexico.

Meanwhile, of course, the United States had become engaged in a much larger war. Thousands of Arizonans took part in World War I. A Pima Indian, Matthew Rivers, was the first native of Arizona to lose his life during the war. One of America's memorable aviation aces during the war was Frank Luke, Jr.

The Grand Canyon was made a national park in 1913. The establishment of Grand Canyon National Monument, to the west of the national park, in 1919 expanded the federal preserves in the canyon area. Ten years later Navajo Bridge across Marble Canyon opened. It was the first direct highway link between Arizona and Utah.

In 1934 Arizona fought a "water war" with California, protesting Parker Dam, which was being built to store Colorado River water for shipment to the Pacific Coast. Arizona Governor B.B. Moeur sent National Guard units to prevent construction at Parker. After making this protest, the troops were removed, and later the United States Supreme Court denied Arizona's claims to increased water rights from the Colorado in the future.

In 1937, almost four hundred years after its discovery, the Colorado River was conquered by Buzz Holstrom, the first man to make a solo trip down its wild reaches. In that year, too, the flat top of Shiva Temple in the Grand Canyon was first explored. Those who had thought prehistoric animals might have been preserved on its isolated plateau were disappointed to find that apparently wild creatures came and went constantly from its summit. In 1938 two women became the first of their sex to boat the rapids of the Colorado. The decades that followed brought wars and peace and great growth.

As Arizona approached the 1980s, the enormous influx of new residents, especially older people attracted by the climate, became not only the most important addition but also one of the greatest problems—where to find the water to support such growth.

INDIAN CULTURE TODAY

Today about 100,000 members of fourteen Indian tribes live on nineteen reservations in Arizona, covering 21,500,000 acres (8,700,749 hectares) or 29 percent of the state's total area. Reservation population and area are the largest in the nation.

Because they live together in their own settlements, Arizona's Indians have retained much of their tribal life and customs. However, they are not isolated from modern living. An Indian papoose may still peep from a cradle board on his mother's back, but mother is probably shopping in a modern center. She is also likely to be surrounded by other mothers carrying their babies in the modern version of the cradle board.

48

A Navajo herds sheep in Monument Valley.

NAVAJO

The Navajo people form the largest tribe on the largest reservation in the United States. The Navajo reservation covers the vast northeast corner of Arizona and spills over into Utah and New Mexico.

Many of the Navajo still live in the typical mud-covered hogan with its door facing the east, from where they consider the good spirits come. They tend their flocks as they wander the treeless terrain searching for the scant nourishment that grows there. But things are changing rapidly under a modern and dynamic tribal council.

Scarcely a generation ago the Navajo were among the poorest of the Indian peoples. Today, thanks to oil, gas, and uranium discoveries as well as land management, they have become wealthy. Instead of distributing this income individually, the leaders have prudently invested much of it on long-range improvement of the water supply, business, and industry to create jobs and increase educational opportunities. Millions of dollars have been used for scholarships for the local young people. Thousands attend government schools, while many hundreds more are enrolled in colleges and universities at tribal expense.

49

Indian artists still practice the old crafts with great skill.

Among the best-known Navajo accomplishments are their noteworthy skills in the arts and crafts. Legend says that they learned their weaving skill about 150 years ago through careful study of the crafty spider. To weave a rug or blanket, early Navajo women had to catch and shear the sheep, card and spin the wool, and dye and ball it before the weaving could begin. Weeks were spent in intense effort at the loom, which was generally stretched between two trees. The tapestry technique was used. After the blanket or rug was cleaned with fresh sand, it was ready to be carried to the trading post.

The earliest blankets were probably almost plain. Gradually, many patterns based on the Navajo life and scenery were originated. One of the first Navajo to weave a pattern based on religious ceremonials was medicine man Hosteen Klah. He invoked the protection of the gods against evil spirits in this work by singing a complete nine-day ceremonial chant.

Many Navajo rugs are superbly woven with designs of great creativity and artistry. Of course, as in every endeavor, many are less artistic. Some have been based on such modern-day patterns as soap wrappers or have had the price woven in.

Navajo artisans accomplish beautiful work in silversmithing, with many of their better pieces including turquoise (sometimes called the Indian diamond). Such silver and turquoise jewelry is the

Navajo's proudest possession. Both men and women wear as much of the family wealth as they can.

Navajo rituals, chants, and other music show a high quality of art. Learning the chants and forms of some of the rituals takes as long as twelve years of study and practice. Each complicated chant is designed to give protection or perform some type of cure.

HOPI

The Hopi reservation is surrounded by the Navajo reservation. The Hopi live in compact villages or pueblos that look like townhouses of our modern cities. Some Hopi houses were inherited from their Pueblo ancestors and are centuries old.

Both Navajo and Hopi make sand pictures used in secret ceremonies. The complicated patterns are worked out in sands of many colors collected from the Painted Desert. Other religious ceremonies occupy much of the Hopi's time. One of their best-known dances is the Snake Dance. Only a small portion of this nine-

Sand from the Painted Desert is used to make sand pictures.

day secret ritual is ever presented in public. Kachina dancers wear masks representing the various Hopi gods. The Hopi make Kachina dolls from cottonwood roots. They also do weaving, work in silver, and produce excellent pottery.

A strange Hopi rite is the rite of the eagles. Young Hopi men climb up to eagles' nests and take eaglets. They tie them on the housetops and wash their heads with yucca suds. After the eaglets have been killed, they are carried to their graves in special crevices in the rocks, with solemn ceremonies

The men are the weavers of the Hopi, one of the few if not the only American Indian tribe where this is true. Their fine work includes the weaving of the traditional white dancing kilt. Every Hopi groom weaves a white wedding robe and a ceremonial robe for his bride and also makes buckskin moccasins for her. The women of the clan of the groom's father have a mud fight with the bride on the day before the wedding, because she is taking the groom from them.

ANCIENT YET MODERN

Modern Apache are cattlemen. The men wear typical cowboy outfits, but many women still retain their long tiered skirts of many colors. The Apache are making intensive efforts these days to improve their tourist facilities and attract visitors to their White Mountains resorts. They once excelled in basket making.

The most distinctive Papago craft is kiaha weaving, which is very much like lace. At the bottom of the Grand Canyon, the Havasupai live in almost the same manner as they have for centuries. The typical Hualpai house is a small dome-shaped structure set on four posts. Each year the Hualpai gather together for what they call a Big Cry, in remembrance of those who have died during the past year. The Mojave have a Cry House where the bodies of their dead are brought before cremation and all the people sing. The Mojave language is still very much in use.

Other present-day Indian peoples living in Arizona are the Pima, Paiute, Chemehuevi, Cocopah, Yavapai, Maricopa, Yuma, and

Yaqui. The Yaqui migrated to this country from Mexico only during the last half century, after the Mexican government practically outlawed the tribe. Long ago they accepted the Roman Catholic religion but have brought many of their tribal ceremonies into it.

The Yaqui religious year is climaxed on Good Friday at Pascua, near Tucson, and at Guadalupe, near Phoenix. Many attend in bright and fanciful costumes, with bodies painted, and some wear grotesque masks. Christ meets his death by shooting, and Judas is burned in effigy. Most Yaqui attend both the Catholic and the native churches.

In 1929 the people of Flagstaff invited Indians of all tribes to come to their town for a powwow with plenty of free food and a chance to play games and have races and dances. This has grown to become one of the country's most popular Indian events. A well-liked game is the chicken pull. Riders on little Indian ponies try to grab a sack of sand from the ground while riding at a fast clip. The Hopi stick and stone race is also popular. One of the greatest attractions was the tug-of-war. Teams of hefty Navajo and Mojave women put up strong resistance to one another. The Mojave were especially large and generally used a 300-pound (136-kilogram) "anchor woman." So many disputes came up that the tug had to be abandoned.

MODERN ARIZONA

From a 1940 population of 500,000, the number of Arizona residents is expected to reach 2,225,000 by 1980. The state's population had more than tripled by the 1970s. In only fifteen more years the population will again have almost doubled if the present rate of growth continues.

Even more spectacular has been the growth of Phoenix from a modest city of 106,818 as late as 1950 to the great desert metropolis of the United States with an estimated 1978 population of 705,000, and a total metropolitan population of more than a million. It is probably safe to say that nothing quite like this has ever taken place before in our history, certainly not in such surroundings.

Natural Treasures

GROWING THINGS

Exotic desert plants are among Arizona's most interesting natural treasures. The mighty saguaro cactus (pronounced sa-WAR-o) stretches its stiff and silent form over great acreages of the state. Everything about this plant is designed to help it live in its hostile environment.

After soaking rains, the root system, which spreads below the surface sometimes as much as fifty feet (fifteen meters) in all directions, absorbs great quantities of water. The walls of the saguaro function like accordion pleats; they expand to take up and store this moisture until the plant is puffed and almost round. In dry weather the stored water is used up; the plants take on a wrinkled appearance and the pleats become sharper.

The creamy white clustered saguaro blossoms are the state flower of Arizona. The fruit is bright red, with bright red pulp and black seeds.

Someone has remarked that saguaro near the highway look like giant hitchhikers. A government bulletin says, "Like people in a crowd, the giant cacti are all similar, yet no two exactly alike. Grotesque rather than beautiful, there is a weird feeling of friendliness in each massive, awkward hulk. The imaginative person may find in many of them a strange resemblance to the figures of humans and animals and other objects."

The rare organ-pipe cactus is similar to the saguaro but instead of a main stem a cluster of many arms grows upward to fifteen or twenty feet (four to six meters). When the flutings of the barrel cactus contract in dry weather, they cause the whole plant to bend to the southwest, forming a kind of compass. Many lives have been saved by the water stored in the barrel cactus. Other cacti include Arizona rainbow, hedgehog, fish hook, jumping cholla, prickly pear, staghorn, and teddy bear. Cacti can live for as long as five years without rainfall. The cacti's sharp spines help prevent animals from eating the plants for their stored water. In a spring with good rainfall, some

Saguaro Cacti in the Catalina Mountains.

areas of the desert blaze with bloom of cactus and other flowering plants and trees.

The century plant does not live a hundred years. It grows very slowly until the flowering stem appears, and then this may grow as rapidly as twelve inches (thirty centimeters) in twenty-four hours. The sotol, known as the desert spoon, and the yucca are among the other notable tall flowering plants of the region. The strange Joshua tree (also called Our Lord's Candle) is another rare and interesting desert plant found in Arizona. Despite its name, Joshua tree, it is not a tree but the largest of the yuccas.

From the deserts to the alpine highlands, there is a wonderful profusion of wild flowers, including desert mariposa lily, Arizona poppy, prickly poppy, desert lupine, sand verbena, desert marigold, desert senna, blue-dicks, paper flowers, harebells, paint brush, ground aster, scarlet gilia, lavender penstemon, phlox, pinks, golden columbine, spider flower, and wallflower. Some Arizona flowers are so tiny they are called "stomach plants" because you discover them only by lying on your stomach and looking at them through magnifying glasses—a new world of miniature blossoms.

In addition to more common varieties, many unique trees and shrubs grow in Arizona. The flowering ironwood has been described as a "huge lavender bouquet" during the blooming season. In season, Arizona's state tree, the Palo Verde, stands as a golden mound of bloom. The weird ocotillo (pronounced o-ko-tee-yo) has no leaves in winter or in dry seasons, but in a normal spring it leafs out, and the tips of its spidery limbs are aflame with candlelike flower clusters up to a foot (thirty centimeters) in length.

The desert willow bears orchidlike flowers from April to August. Another flowering tree is the acacia. The brittle bush has a brilliant yellow flower, and the cliff rose is an evergreen with large cream-colored blossoms. The humming bird bush is covered with long scarlet blossoms. One of the most conspicuous shrubs is the creosote bush. After rain showers it gives off a pungent, tarry smell. In deep soil the mesquites form dense forests of large trees in many parts of Arizona.

Most of Arizona's larger trees grow at altitudes above 5,000 feet (1,524 meters). Ponderosa and limber pine, Douglas and white fir, Engelmann spruce, aspen, Arizona cypress, piñon pine, junipers,

Barrel Cacti bloom from July through September.

locust, gambel oak, tesota, cottonwood, walnut, and sycamore are all found. The only native palm tree of Arizona is the *Washingtonia Arizonica*. Only a few of these now grow in Palm Canyon.

The Arizona Development Board estimates that there are almost 20 million acres of forest in Arizona, a very large part of this in national forests.

No description of Arizona trees and plants would be complete without mention of the tumbleweed. This famous plant breaks away from its roots in autumn and hurtles across the windy land.

"ALL GOD'S CREATURES"

One of the smallest of Arizona animals is among the most interesting. The pack rat, or trade rat, is a thief. It will steal any article it can run off with but thoughtfully replaces the stolen piece with a pine cone, a stick, or chunk of cactus. Many unsolved Arizona mysteries are probably due to pack rats. On one occasion a miner missed some sticks of dynamite. Jumping a stream, he almost landed on the stolen dynamite, carried off and hidden by the pack rats. In another instance, a surveying project almost failed when a pack rat made off with the only ruler the surveyors had. And three prospectors nearly dissolved their partnership before they discovered the thefts in their camp had been carried out by pack rats instead of each other.

Hunters rank the following animals as the most popular of Arizona sport: javelina (a kind of wild pig), bighorn sheep, elk, mountain lion, black bear, white-tail deer, mule deer, turkey, buffalo, and pronghorn antelope. Arizona has the largest population of mule deer in the country, estimated at more than fifty thousand. Elk became extinct in Arizona but they were reintroduced on the Mogollon Plateau.

Many Arizona men have gained great reputations as hunters of the mountain lion. Other members of the cat family found in Arizona's forested areas are bobcats and ocelots.

Herds of wild horses and wild burros may still be found in parts of

57

*The pack rat and the golden eagle are
among Arizona's natural treasures.*

the state. The desert fox is noted for his long ears, and its relative the coyote is so sly and clever that its numbers increase despite great eradication efforts. Some hunters insist that coyotes know when a person is carrying a gun; they show no fear when a person is carrying only a stick.

A number of unusual reptiles are found in Arizona, including the only poisonous lizard in the United States—the Gila monster. The horned lizard (called horned toad) has become so popular as a pet that this gentle animal is threatened with extinction. The chuckawalla, an edible lizard, and the Uta are probably the most common lizards in the state. The king snake is respected because it is immune to rattlesnake venom and frequently attacks and devours the poisonous snake.

Tarantulas have been known to reach a size of six inches (fifteen centimeters) across, but they do not live up to their formidable reputation. Their bite is said to be usually about as serious as a bee sting.

At least 60 percent of all species of birds and animals found in America have been sighted in Arizona. These include 400 varieties of birds, 150 of them permanent residents. Among the birds are such different species as pelicans, wild turkeys, and golden and bald eagles. Even such exotic birds as thick-billed parrots inhabit the Chiricahua Mountains.

The rare Arizona native trout is found nowhere else, and fishermen catch other kinds of trout and several of bass. Channel catfish, bluegills, crappies, and sunfish are also important game fish.

MINERALS

Gold, silver, copper, iron, graphite, gypsum, lithium, barite, cement, clays, feldspar, fluorspar, lime, brucite, niobium (tantalum), scoria, thorium, talc, manganese, mercury, mica, molybdenum, perlite, pumice, sand and gravel, silica, stone, tungsten, uranium, and vanadium are some of the minerals and natural resources of Arizona.

The mining, cutting, and polishing of gem stones is the oldest mineral craft in Arizona. Turquoise, obsidian, and other stones were used for ornament centuries before the Europeans came. Arizona's unusual variety of gems also includes amethyst, garnet, peridot, topaz, beryl, onyx, agate, opal, tourmaline, quartz, chalcedony, dumortierite, and petrified wood.

Of all the minerals, however, one is without question the most precious of all—water. Even states with adequate rainfall are concerned about running out of water in the not too distant future. In Arizona the assurance of proper use and conservation of every drop of water is absolutely essential. Most of Arizona's water comes from underground supplies, though some is supplied by storage lakes created by dams.

The first artesian well was created by the Mormons at St. David in 1887. Although Arizona is "one of the most efficient users of water in the world," there is a large loss each year of permanent and dependable water supply. This loss results from water being pumped from ground deposits much faster than it is replaced. In a few years the water deposits possibly of centuries have been taken from the ground.

Many plans for overcoming the water scarcity have been considered. Some of those are based on the rapidly growing ability to turn sea water into fresh water. Another is called the Central Arizona Project, with plans to bring water from the Colorado River.

People Use Their Treasures

BURIED TREASURE—LOST AND FOUND

The oldest commercial activity in Arizona and the one that has contributed the most romantic legends is mining. Copper has been the major mining product. In little more than a century, between 1860 and 1963, almost $8 billion worth of copper was produced in Arizona. Modern copper mining began in 1855 in the Ajo district, where both high-grade and low-grade ores were found. In the 1870s some of the world's most valuable high-grade copper ore was found in Arizona.

Great mining companies were begun, including the Arizona Copper Company and Detroit Copper Company in the Clifton and Morenci district; the Copper Queen of Phelps Dodge and the Calumet and Arizona in the Bisbee area; Old Dominion Mining and Smelting Company in the Globe region; and the United Verde at Jerome. Gradually the Phelps Dodge Company gained ownership or control of most of these and became the most influential corporation in the state and one of the largest producers of copper in the country.

By the 1900s, high-grade copper ore in Arizona was decreasing rapidly; there were vast amounts of lower-grade ore, but its use was not possible. In 1906 a young engineer, J.C. Jackling, developed new methods of extracting copper from low-grade ore. Now some companies can show a profit by working ore from which only twelve pounds (five kilograms) of copper can be extracted from every ton of ore.

By 1907 Arizona became the leading copper producer in the United States, and has not given up the leadership in any year since that time. Today the state also leads in total production of all metals except iron. Yearly value of minerals in Arizona is about one and a half billion dollars.

The most glamorous metals, gold and silver, have been the second and third most valuable minerals in Arizona over the years. From

Opposite: Bisbee is a living legend of the state's mining history.

1893 to 1900 numerous new gold deposits were discovered in the Bradshaw Mountains, north of Tucson, and in the desert of Yuma County. Now gold is produced as a by-product of copper mining.

The stories of the rugged prospectors who roamed the hills searching doggedly for gold or silver and of the unusual way strikes were made have added much to the folklore of Arizona. The great strike at Rich Hill came about because a prospecting party went out of their way to find a straying donkey. Miners who hurried into the region are said to have scraped out a million dollars of gold in this region within a month, using little more than butcher knives. While the total probably has been exaggerated, the discovery greatly accelerated mineral exploration in Arizona.

Another animal, Henry Wickenburg's burro, is said to have been responsible for the greatest Arizona gold discovery. The animal strayed off. Wickenburg became so angry he threw stones at the stubborn creature; when he discovered how heavy the stones were, he had them analyzed, and the Vulture Mine was the result.

Shorty Alger was prospecting in the Harcuvar Mountains. When he slipped on a slope, he struck his prospector's pick into the ground to break his fall. Drawing it out he found a gold nugget stuck on the end that later proved to weigh more than half a pound (about a quarter of a kilogram).

Bustling or booming communities grew up across the state as the various mining discoveries were made. Most of these became the tough mining towns of the wildest tradition of the West. Names like Bisbee and Tombstone have become legends. As processing plants grew up, the sounds of ore stamping machines could be heard day and night. As one prospector said, "That's the music I like to hear, pounding out gold and silver. There ain't no brass bands like it."

Many towns grew to populations in the hundreds or thousands; then, as the minerals gave out, the people left, adding to the many ghost towns of Arizona such names as Silver King, Oatman, Gila City, La Paz, Walker, Charleston, Cerbat, Octave, White Hills, Gold Road, Oro Blanco, Pearce, McCabe, Ehrenberg, Weaver, Humboldt, Helvetia, Vulture City, Duquesne, and Jerome. All hold fascinating stories of success and tragedy.

Many Arizona tales concern the mines and fortunes that became "lost" in one way or another. Probably the most repeated lost-mine legend anywhere is the fabled Lost Dutchman mine in the Superstition Mountains east of Phoenix. One of the many versions of this story began with a young Mexican who found a fabulously wealthy gold mine in the region. Because the area would soon become a part of the United States through the Gadsden Purchase, the young man brought to the mine almost the entire population of his Mexican community. Returning on the long trip from the Superstitions, they took out as much gold as they could carry. However, on the homeward journey all but two boys were killed by the Apache.

When they were older, the two boys rediscovered the mine, but were killed by Jacob Waltz, or Wolz, known as The Dutchman, and Wolz took over the mine. When other prospectors followed him and tried to find his wealth, he killed them. Tradition says that he murdered eight men to keep the secret of his wealth. When Wolz died he left instructions on how to get to the mine, but no one has ever been able to find his landmarks.

Thousands have tried to locate the Lost Dutchman mine ever since. Some have died of thirst or lost their way; others say they have been shot at; some have returned after the most awful hardships. A tradition has grown that the mountains are cursed. Mining experts dismiss the legend as fiction, pointing out that the Superstitions are only lightly mineralized.

Another famous lost mine—The Escalante—is said to have been in the Santa Catalina Mountains. Father Escalante, an assistant to Father Kino, supposedly worked the mine, storing the refined gold behind an iron door. When the Apache wiped out the little community, all traces of the mine and the iron door were lost. The only person who really found a gold mine in the story was Harold Bell Wright, who wrote a book called *The Mine with the Iron Door.*

Today's visitors to Arizona may obtain a map telling them where to begin their search for the Lost Silver of Pish-la-ki, Lost Nugget Mine, Organ Grinders Lost-Ledge, Lost Quartz of Tonto Apaches, Lost Mountain of Silver, and Lost Sopori Mine among others.

Arizona contains other valuable minerals and natural resources.

They are, in order of value, zinc, sand and gravel, lead, cement, molybdenum, building stone, uranium, lime, clay, and manganese. Mercury, tungsten, vanadium, asbestos, barite, feldspar, fluorspar, gypsum, mica, perlite, pumice, silica, and sodium sulfate are also produced. It is interesting to note that the famous New York jewelry house of Tiffany once owned an Arizona turquoise mine.

Mineral production brings Arizona about $1.5 billion each year.

THE PEOPLE WORK

Cotton is by far the most important agricultural crop in Arizona. Today it makes up almost a third of the state's agricultural income. In 1903, when Secretary of Agriculture James Wilson's experts went into all parts of the world searching for new farm crops, they brought back cotton from Egypt that grew with a much longer fiber. Tested in the Salt River Valley, this long-staple cotton proved as suitable for Arizona as it had been for Egypt. Arizona cotton growers have been improving its quality and production ever since.

Because of its lettuce and other salad ingredients, Arizona has been called the Salad Bowl of the Nation; $100 million worth of lettuce alone is grown each year in the state. Alfalfa and hay, melons, citrus fruits, cabbage, carrots, broccoli, barley, and onions are other important crops. Dates, also first brought in by the United States Department of Agriculture experts, are considered the most "picturesque" crop in Arizona. They are carefully pollinated by hand. The taller trees contain permanent platforms for pollinating and harvesting, and clusters of ripening dates are protected from dust and insects by plastic or cheesecloth bags.

Livestock production has been increasing steadily in Arizona, but it has not yet passed crops in state farm income. Total farm income in Arizona exceeds $1 billion per year.

In the period from the late 1960s to the late 1970s, the value of manufactured products from Arizona more than doubled. It now surpasses $2 billion per year. Principal products are electrical equipment, primary metals, and machinery other than electrical products.

64

The "working ranch" is still a prominent part of the Arizona scene.

TRANSPORTATION AND COMMUNICATION

Many modes of transportation—for both people and goods—have been utilized in Arizona. These include *carritas,* camels, river steamers, wagons, twenty-four-mule teams, and stagecoaches.

Because of its deserts, Edward F. Beale felt that camels should do well as pack animals. Camels were brought in from the Near East. They carried heavy loads, swam streams, climbed icy mountains, and did jobs no other animal could do, but other animals feared just the sight of them. After the Civil War, some were abandoned and roamed free across the deserts. Sometimes at night, the ghostly silhouette of a camel could be seen on top of a dune. Gradually, however, they were killed or died out.

When the first steamboat came up the Colorado River on what became a much-used freight route, the Indians yelled that the devil was coming, blowing fire from his nose and kicking up the water with his feet.

The Southern Pacific Railroad was ready in 1877 to bring the first railroad into Arizona across the Colorado at Yuma. Suddenly, the federal government refused permission for trains to cross into the military reservation over the new bridge the railroad had built. However, train engineers slipped a train across in defiance of the government order, to bring the first train to Arizona, before they were quickly forced back. When permission was granted construction resumed, and the first train reached Tucson in March 1880. The first railroad to cross the state was completed in 1881.

The *Weekly Arizonian,* begun in 1859 at Tubac, was the first newspaper published in Arizona. *The Epitaph,* of Tombstone, was well known, if for no other reason than its appropriate name.

Arizona has gained renown in a unique field of journalism. Its highway department publishes one of the nation's unusual magazines, *Arizona Highways.* People in almost every country subscribe, and even those who live far away become familiar with the state's crannies and back roads by reading and looking at *Arizona Highways.* The magazine is particularly noted for the beauty of its full-color illustrations showing the wonderful scenery and variety of the state.

As might be expected, the tourist industry is one of the most important activities in Arizona. Tourists spend more than $1 billion per year in the state.

THE WATER OF LIFE

The use and conservation of water are thoroughly and carefully carried on in Arizona. Ever since prehistoric times water has been brought from the rivers for use of the people. Some of the world's greatest dams are a part of the state's water system. These include the mighty Hoover Dam and the even more mighty Glen Canyon Dam, which contains a third more concrete than Hoover Dam.

Other important dams include Imperial, Parker, Davis, Bartlett,

Roosevelt Dam as seen from Apache Trail.

Horseshoe, Laguna, Horse Mesa, Mormon Flat, Stewart Mountain, Carl Pleasant, Theodore Roosevelt, and Coolidge. Calvin Coolidge dedicated his namesake in 1930, and humorist Will Rogers spoke. The San Carlos Reservoir had hardly begun to fill behind the dam when Rogers looked at the grass in the bottom and said, "If this was my lake, I'd mow it."

Agriculture is the principal user of irrigated water in Arizona. More than a million acres (four hundred thousand hectares) of land are irrigated today, requiring about two-thirds of all water used in the state.

The people of Arizona are acutely aware of the fact that "Assured water means a stable Arizona."

Human Treasures

THEY LED THE WAY

The first person to bring European civilization to what is now Arizona, of course, was Father Eusebio Francisco Kino, a native of Austria who had his headquarters at Mission Nuestra Senora de los Dolores in Sonora, Mexico. He spent most of the years from 1692 to 1711 traveling over the vast and hostile reaches of northern Mexico and Arizona. During most of his time in this wilderness region, he had only a few soldiers as protection as he went about establishing missions in Arizona and Mexico, braving thirst and scorching heat, the cold of winter, and sometimes hostile Indians. He baptized thousands of Indians, taught them how to raise crops, and introduced them to methods of raising livestock.

Noted also as an explorer and geographer, he opened Arizona's most famous (and "worst") road—El Camino del Diablo, the Devil's Highway, across the southwest corner of what is now the state. He also reached the Colorado River and thus established the fact that California was not an island, a belief held until that time. He wrote *Historical Memoir of Pimeria Alta,* a valuable description of Arizona.

Like Father Kino, Father Francisco Tomas Garcés had a deep love for the Papago and Pima Indians and willingly underwent numerous hardships to serve the people. The most famous journey took him on a mission to the Hopi Indians through 2,500 miles (4,023 kilometers) of Arizona country, where he came in contact with twenty-five thousand Indians.

One of the first to make the difficult climb down the Grand Canyon wall, Father Garcés visited the Havasupai Indians in 1776 and saw a great river flowing red with the soil it carried. He gave it the name Colorado ("red colored"). The Hopi, however, rejected his message and would not permit him to remain.

Garcés was one of a party who had the vision to blaze a trail from Pimeria Alta to the Colorado River, where he stopped. The others went on to the Spanish missions on the Pacific. Father Garcés was killed in 1781 trying to bring Christianity to the Yuma Indians.

68

Diorama of Father Kino at Tumacacori National Monument.

Charles D. Poston has been known as the Father of Arizona. After being shipwrecked in the Gulf of California, Poston and Herman Ehrenberg reopened an old silver mine near Tubac. Poston later headed a million-dollar exploring and mining company. When United States troops left the region during the Civil War, Poston moved to Washington, where he was one of the persons responsible for the granting of territorial status to Arizona. He was named superintendent of Indian affairs for Arizona and later was the territory's delegate to Congress.

During travels in Asia, Poston became interested in a cult of sun worshipers and later built a road at his own expense to the top of what he called Parsee Butte (now Poston's Butte), near Florence. At the top he built a tomb, intended to be part of a temple to the sun, that was never completed. The project became known locally as Poston's Folly. Poston served in many governmental posts and died in Phoenix in 1902. He is buried beneath a monument on Poston's Butte.

TOUGH HOMBRES

Bill Williams, for whom an Arizona town, river, and mountain were named, began his career at seventeen as a Missouri circuit rider. He lived for more than ten years with the Osage Indians, then plunged into the wilderness to become a mountaineer. W.H. Robinson described him: "He was the typical plainsman of the dime novel. He always rode an Indian pony, and his Mexican stirrups were big as coal scuttles. His buckskin suit was bedaubed with grease until it had the appearance of polished leather; his feet were never encased in anything but moccasins, and his buckskin trousers had the traditional fringe on the outer seam. Naturally, Indian signs were an open book to him, and he was even readier to take a scalp than an Apache." He was killed in Colorado by the Ute, who were once his friends, because he had turned against them.

Pete Kitchen arrived in Arizona in 1854. According to Frank C. Lockwood: "During the bloodiest days of Indian warfare, his name was a household word among the white settlers. . . . His hacienda, on the summit of a rocky hill . . . was as much a fort as a ranch-house. . . . Pete Kitchen was the only settler whom the Apaches could not dislodge. They made raid after raid, and shot his pigs so full of arrows that they looked like 'walking pin cushions.' They killed or drove out his bravest neighbors; they killed his herder; and they slaughtered his stepson; but Pete Kitchen fought on undaunted. His name struck terror to every Apache heart; and at last, finding that he was too tough a nut to crack, they passed him by."

70

In front of Pete Kitchen's ranch house today is the boot-hill cemetery where he buried the outlaws and desperados he killed. His wife faithfully burned candles over their graves for the souls of those killed by her husband.

Another great Arizona Indian fighter was King Woolsey. His ruthlessness, strength, courage, and cunning proved more than equal to the Indians in all his meetings with them.

Al Sieber, one of Arizona's best-known scouts, was nicknamed Man of Iron. He was called on for some of the most difficult government work in frontier history, controlling relentless Apache when no one else could. In his older years he fell on hard times, with no help from the government he served so well. He worked on the construction of the Theodore Roosevelt Dam. After some rocks had been blasted, a heavy stone was perched in such a way that it could fall on his Apache work crew. Sieber managed to knock the rock away but he was crushed to death, saving the men of the tribe he fought so bitterly in earlier years. With their own hands, the Apache laborers erected a monument to Sieber's memory on the spot where he died.

The deputy United States marshal at Tombstone, Wyatt Earp, gained notoriety in his own day and then became even better known through a fictionalized television series. According to legend, he single-handedly held off three hundred miners who wanted to lynch a prisoner. In fact, the Earp brothers did not have a very good reputation locally, but the Earp name has been greatly glamorized in later stories.

Some of Arizona's most colorful characters were outlaws. Curly Bill Brocius was a handsome bandit who dressed like a movie villain. He delighted in robbing the rich and included one deputy sheriff among his friends. The deputy sent Bill to collect taxes, and no one ever refused to pay.

On one occasion Curly Bill and his men stole a locomotive and ran it up and down the tracks with the engineer and crew in pursuit. At another time, Curly and his gang boarded a train carrying evangelist Dwight L. Moody and his vocal soloist. According to one account the outlaw addressed the preacher, "Mr. Moody, we know you ain't got time to preach me an' the boys a sermon ... but we would like to

Frontier Town, Old Tucson.

hear Mr. Sankey sing 'Pull for the Shore.' '' When Sankey refused, Curly drew out his six shooter, and Sankey sang. The report says that when the song was finished the outlaws drank to their health with some beer and shook hands all around.

Johnny Ringo, Johnny-Behind-the-Deuce, the Clantons, and many other outlaws fought, robbed, rode, searched for gold, and gambled in the picturesque past of the Arizona frontier.

CREATIVE SPIRITS

Most of the art and literature inspired by and in Arizona has reflected the life and climate of the region.

The Cowboy by Ross Santee is said to be an ''authentic story of life on the open range.'' This work was illustrated by the author himself.

Oliver La Farge won the Pulitzer Prize for fiction in 1930 for *Laughing Boy,* based on his years of study of Arizona Indian life. Owen Wister and Harold Bell Wright both spent much time in the state.

The first nationally known Arizona humorist was Dick Wick Hall, who published the *Salome Sun.* He made popular the slogan "Salome—where she danced." With the hot desert sands of Arizona in mind, Hall wrote: "Everybody seems to think I'm the man that made Salome dance, but it wasn't my fault at all. I told her to keep her shoes on or the sand would burn her feet." At another time he wrote: "Melons don't do very well here becuz the vines grow so fast they wear the melons out dragging them around the ground—and in dry years we sometimes have to plant onions in between the rows of potatoes and then scratch the onions to made the potatoes eyes water enough to irrigate the rest of the garden—and the kids sure do hate to scratch the onions on moonlight nights."

Artist Thomas Moran painted the Grand Canyon, and his work *The Chasm of the Colorado* occupies a conspicuous spot in the Capitol at Washington. Frederic Remington did much of his famed Western painting in Arizona, and several of the state's Indians have gained excellent reputations in crafts or in art. One of these is Fred Kabotie, a leading Hopi artist.

One of the best descriptions of the Grand Canyon is found in the music of Ferde Grofé's *Grand Canyon Suite.*

SUCH INTERESTING PEOPLE

Twenty-one-year-old Congressional Medal of Honor winner Frank Luke, Jr., was known as the Balloon Buster for his work against German observation balloons and aircraft in World War I. He received official credit for twenty-one victories in his short thirty-nine days of combat. He fought as a lone eagle and often disregarded regulations and discipline. With his engine dead and plane riddled with bullets, Luke was shot down and killed behind enemy lines.

In the field of public service, Carl Hayden served in the United States Congress continually from Arizona statehood until his retirement in 1972. Lewis W. Douglas, native of Arizona, gained an international reputation as United States Ambassador to Great Britain. In 1962 Douglas donated the historic Douglas home at Jerome to the state, and it is now a state park. George W.P. Hunt, the first elected state governor of Arizona, served seven terms.

Until his death in 1934 he was regarded by many as "the most influential man in Arizona's political life." Hunt often said he arrived at Globe in 1881 driving a burro, served as a waiter in a Chinese restaurant, and worked in the almost suffocating mines. Eventually he became Globe's leading merchant and a banker and finally entered politics.

Barry Goldwater, born in Arizona when it was still a territory, became a United States Senator and stirred worldwide controversy during his campaign as the Republican candidate for president in 1964.

Joe Drew kept a station on the old stage route in the desert at Culling's Well. One night a man staggered to his door almost dead from thirst. From far out on the desert he had seen the light in Drew's window. Drew put up a tall pole the next night, and for many years kept a light burning at its top to guide any wanderers. He became known as Keeper of the Desert Lighthouse.

Pauline Cushman of Florence served for a short time as a spy in the Civil War. When captured, Confederate forces were about to execute her, but they had to abandon her during a retreat. President Lincoln commended her for her services. She was widely advertised as a lecturer. In later life she moved to San Francisco, where she lived in poverty until finally committing suicide.

One of Arizona's most colorful characters, Henry Wickenburg, discovered the Vulture Mine in 1863 and the town of Wickenburg grew up around the mine. For a time it was one of the largest cities in the state; it missed by only two votes being selected as capital of Arizona. Wickenburg operated a small farm near the town. When his land was ruined by sand and silt brought in after Walnut Grove Dam collapsed, Wickenburg became discouraged. On his eighty-eighth birthday (in 1905), he wandered into the mesquite grove near his house and shot himself.

Teaching and Learning

Climate, surroundings, faculty, and opportunities for field work have combined to make the University of Arizona one of the nation's fastest growing major universities. Science, electrical engineering, fine arts, astronomy, and Oriental studies have experienced rapid growth at the university.

In 1855 the territorial legislature provided for a college system that would include a university if the citizens of Tucson would give forty acres (sixteen hectares) for a campus within a certain time. Just before the time elapsed, several leading gamblers donated desert land a mile (1.6 kilometers) from town, and the university was established in 1890. Now the university is almost in the heart of the city. It is considered to be one of the most beautiful and unusual campuses in America.

Early fame came to the university through the work of Professor A.E. Douglas, who perfected the method of dating prehistoric ruins by a study of the tree ring growth in beams taken from ruins.

The oldest institution of higher education in the state is Arizona State University at Tempe, opened in 1886. It also is noted for the increasing size of both its facilities and its student body. Northern Arizona University at Flagstaff is another fine state-operated institution.

The American Graduate School of International Management near Glendale offers unique courses preparing students in banking, commerce, sales, and marketing.

Taliesin West, northeast of Phoenix, was founded by Frank Lloyd Wright for the preparation of architects.

Two of the world's outstanding centers of astronomical research are Lowell Observatory at Flagstaff and Kitt Peak National Observatory, southwest of Tucson.

Astronomer Percival Lowell predicted, on the basis of his studies that a new planet would be found farthest out in the solar system. Fourteen years after Dr. Lowell died, Clyde W. Tombaugh of the Lowell Observatory discovered a planet where Lowell had predicted, and named this planet Pluto. This is recognized as one of the great

discoveries of modern astronomy. The observatory was also first to describe the theory that the universe is expanding. It was first to determine the temperature of Mars, Jupiter, Saturn, and Venus, and is particularly noted for its study of Mars.

Kitt Peak was selected as the location for another observatory after 150 possible mountain sites had been studied in one of the most careful searches in the history of science. It was chosen for its clear air, temperature stability, and low wind velocity. The Papago Indians, on whose reservation the peak rises, were reluctant to lease the ground. However, after the awed tribal council looked at the heavens through the Steward Telescope at the University of Arizona, they agreed to let "the men with the long eyes" lease their land for Kitt Peak National Observatory.

On Kitt Peak now stands one of the world's strangest structures, the most powerful solar telescope ever built. An 80-inch (203-centimeter) mirror on a concrete tower reflects sunlight down a 500-foot (152-meter) shaft, that slants deep into the ground for 300 feet (91 meters). An extraordinary program at the observatory deals with the study of galaxies, stars, and nebulae and the overall plan for putting a space telescope into orbit.

The earliest formal education in Arizona was provided by the priests in mission schools. When these were abandoned in 1827, there was no formal education in Arizona until early territorial days, when the school at Mission San Xavier del Bac was reopened. The population was too small and scattered for schools. John Spring opened a public school at Tucson in 1871 for 138 boys, almost all Mexican. At any instant the pupils and teacher in this school might expect to be scattered by an Indian raid. Governor A.P.K. Stafford worked from 1869 to 1877 persuading the state legislature to establish schools. In recognition for his efforts, Governor Stafford became known as the Father of the Public School System in Arizona.

Opposite: Arizona State University, Tempe.

Enchantment of Arizona

The picturesque quality of Arizona results not only from the state's unsurpassed natural wonders but also from the many rich ethnic and religious backgrounds, activities, and cultures of its people, including Mormons, Catholics, cowboys, prospectors, soldiers, miners, Confederates, Yankees, Indians, Mexicans, blacks, Serbians, Italians, English, Spanish, and many others.

SAND, SAGUAROS, AND SOPHISTICATION— SOUTHERN ARIZONA

Those who think of southern Arizona only as a land where spirited little dust devils whirl across endless stretches of sand, where buzzards circle in lazy flight, and coyotes pause to watch passing autos are in for many surprises.

The graceful ruins of Tumacacori National Mounment on the site of an ancient Indian village are reminders of civilizations that inhabited the region many centuries ago. Even more remarkable is the beautiful mission of San Xavier del Bac. The present building, started in 1768, is still in use as a church. The oldest mission in the country still serving the Indians, it has been called an "architectural miracle." Adobe statues of a cat and mouse face each other on top of the mission's façade. Indian legends claim that when the cat catches the mouse the end of the world will come.

Passage of Coronado's great expedition is remembered in Coronado National Memorial, between Bisbee and Nogales. Coronado Peak affords visitors a spectacular view of both the United States and Mexico.

Many reminders of the mining history and the Apache raids are found throughout the region.

Bisbee is one of the few nonferrous mining communities to surpass a billion dollars in value of ore produced, and the region con-

Opposite: Civic Center, Tucson.

tinues to be one of the most important metal producers in the entire country. Bisbee is two miles (three kilometers) long, stretching up Mule Pass Gulch, but only a few blocks wide.

Between Bisbee and Tombstone are the Mule Mountains, named for two peaks shaped like mule ears. This region is said to be one of the most beautiful desert-mountain areas anywhere.

Tombstone, once a rip-roaring mining town, claims to be the "town too tough to die." It lives on as a tourist and health center and winter resort. The once lusty Bird Cage theater is now a museum, and Boothill Cemetery is the last resting place of characters great and small, good and bad. An unexpected distinction of Tombstone is the claim that it possesses the world's largest rose tree, with a trunk 72 inches (183 centimeters) around.

To the east are the Chiricahua Mountains, once haunts of the Chiricahua Apache. Seventeen square miles (forty-four square kilometers) of the region are now the Chiricahua National Monument, a wonderland of tortuous canyons and innumerable rock sculptures. One mountain, Cochise Head, forms a striking silhouette of an Indian face, with noble forehead, Roman nose, and jutting chin.

Another wonderland of rocks is found in Texas Canyon.

Near the present site of St. David, the Mormon Battalion was attacked by wild bulls. In the battle that lasted from early morning until noon one or two Mormons were injured; several pack animals and at least sixty bulls were killed.

The Arizona livestock industry began when Father Kino imported cattle for the Pima Indians about 1700. They were typical Mexican cattle with long icepick-sharp horns. Nogales is a popular point of entry into Mexico, and only a fence separates the two countries at this point. Two of the world's most unusual plant life preserves, Saguaro National Monument and Organ Pipe Cactus National Monument, are located in southern Arizona. The rare organ-pipe is found only in this vicinity in the United States, and it is preserved in 518 square miles (1,342 square kilometers) of unspoiled desert area. In May and June the organ-pipe cacti are spectacular with white, pink, and lavender blossoms. Other cacti in bloom, golden poppy, blue lupine, and other flowers make a garden of much of the desert in springtime.

In Saguaro National Monument, these fantastic giant cacti grow as tall as fifty feet (fifteen meters). More than twenty-five other types of cacti grow there also. Visitors sometimes wonder at finding a woody mass on the desert floor, in the shape of wooden shoes. These knotty substances are formed inside the saguaro by woodpeckers boring in to make a nest. The cactus covers the hole with a hard fiber; when the plant dies these shoelike fiber masses remain.

Many archeologists consider the Casa Grande (Big House) ruins to be the most interesting prehistoric structure in all southern Arizona. Lieutenant Juan Manje visited Casa Grande with Father Kino in 1697 and described it: " . . . a large edifice whose principal room in the middle is of four stories . . . made of strong cement and clay . . . so smooth on the inside that they resemble planed boards and so polished that they shine like pueblo pottery. The angles of the windows, which are square, are very true." The Casa Grande ruins are now a national monument.

Yuma, the center of one of Arizona's largest irrigated areas, is the largest city in southwestern Arizona. The first ferry boat to travel across the Colorado River here is said to have been made in Michigan, drawn across the continent as a prairie schooner, and floated down the Gila River to the Colorado. The first European child born in Arizona was born on this raft as it floated downstream. Today, the dunes near Yuma are popular spots for desert location shots of motion picture companies.

OLD PUEBLO—NEW TUCSON

Almost twelve hundred years ago a prehistoric tribe established a village called Stjukson, meaning "village of the dark spring at the foot of the mountain." Modern Tucson took both its name and its site from the old village when it was established in 1776.

Tucson today is a growing metropolis famous for its healthful climate and increasing number of cultural activities. The University of

Arizona contains many of these attractions. On the campus are the College of Fine Arts Theater and Museum, the Geological Museum, and the University Art Galleries. The Arizona State Museum, also located on campus, is a treasure house of the ancient life of the Southwest, including exhibits of ten thousand years of life in the region.

Tucson's Sunday Evening Forum is the largest community forum in the United States. In music, the Tucson Arizona Boys' Chorus and the Tucson Symphony are well known.

The drive from the valley floor up Mount Lemmon has been called "one of the most exciting drives in the world." Another spectacle is the view of Tucson at night from Sentinel Peak, with the shimmering city lights sparkling in the clear air.

Tucson Mountain Park is noted for Arizona-Sonora Desert Museum, one of the country's most unusual zoos. It features creatures and botanical specimens of the plains, deserts, and Arizona mountains. There is a unique underground tunnel where visitors can see the life of burrowing animals. The museum acquires seventy thousand mealy worms and one thousand crickets a month to feed its snakes, centipedes, scorpions, and other insect eaters. The prairie dog village is very popular, and the bat cave is eerie but fascinating.

Mountain Park also houses Old Tucson Village. It was built for a movie set to depict Tucson as it was in the 1860s. Now a Western-style amusement park is being developed from it. Another relic of the past is Fort Lowell, near Tucson, now partially restored.

La Fiesta de Los Vaqueros, the Tucson rodeo, highlights the winter season. It provides four action-packed days of championship performers and a 1-mile-long (1.6 kilometers) all-horse-drawn-vehicle rodeo parade.

CENTRAL ARIZONA

The streets of Globe are often crowded with colorful figures, Apache men and women, cowboys, and tourists trying to outdo each other in their appearance. This mining town is still flourishing in

Fun and adventure are found at Slide Rock Oak Creek Canyon near Sedona.

modern days. Globe took its name from a spherical boulder of almost solid silver containing markings on its surface that looked vaguely like continents of a world globe. Another interesting natural feature is the silhouette of a "sleeping beauty" made by mountains near Globe. Gila Pueblo in Six Shooter Canyon near Globe contains the Southwest Archeological Center of the U.S. Department of the Interior. Another interesting ruin is Besh-ba-Gowah.

Coolidge Dam is the largest multiple-dome dam ever built. Arizona humorist Reg Manning said the domes resemble three bald-headed men.

Apache Leap commemorates the legend of an Indian tragedy. Seventy-five Apache warriors forced to the edge of this cliff near Superior jumped to their death rather than surrender.

More than ten thousand species of plant life from every continent add to the interest of Southwestern Arboretum, near Superior.

Many interesting sights of central Arizona are reached by the Apache Trail, which circles to the north of Superstition Mountain. Theodore Roosevelt said, "The Apache Trail combines the grandeur of the Alps, the glory of the Rockies, and the magnificence of the Grand Canyon, and then adds an indefinable something that none of the others has. To me it is the most awe-inspiring and most sublimely beautiful panorama nature has ever created." Canyon Lake, Apache Lake, and the gaping chasm of Fish Creek Canyon are all located along the road.

Huge rock temples rise more than a thousand feet (more than three hundred meters) from the floor of Fish Creek Canyon, almost half a mile (nearly one kilometer) below the canyon rim. Visitors are awed by the view of this gorge from the drive along the bottom. Theodore Roosevelt Dam and Lake may also be seen from the Apache Trail. Nearby Tonto National Monument preserves the ancient Salado cliff dwellings. In the White Mountains stands Kinishba Ruin, with more than seven hundred rooms. Fourteen types of pottery have been found there. Some bowls contain a glaze almost never found in such ruins. The largest part of this vast archeological treasure is still to be explored.

A point of interest in west-central Arizona is Parker Dam and the town of Parker. Near Quertyite is the grave of Hi Jolly, whose real name was Hadji Ali. He had been brought from his Syria to drive the camels used as pack animals before the Civil War. When the camels were no longer used, Hadji became one of the area's most picturesque prospectors. His grave is topped with a copper camel.

Mesa, one of the largest of the Phoenix suburbs, was founded by the Mormons in 1878. It was laid out with wide streets to accommodate wagons pulled by many yoke of oxen or long strings of mules and horses. The Mormon Temple at Mesa has been called "one of the most beautiful ecclesiastical structures in the nation." It is said to resemble the temple of Solomon. The gardens are among the most beautiful in the state, with a reflecting pool bordered with flowers from the gate to the main temple entrance.

IN THE VALLEY OF THE SUN—PHOENIX

Phoenix offers the visitor an "almost incredible panorama in the desert" and claims to provide "everything under the sun" for his comfort and enjoyment.

In a hundred years the capitol building has progressed from a tent at original Fort Whipple to a fine structure built of native Arizona materials. The winged statue atop the dome holds a torch for liberty and a wreath for peace. It was completed in 1900. Two wings were added in 1918 and 1939. In 1960 new senate and house of representatives buildings were added to the capitol complex. In the ten-acre (four-hectare) grounds are many varieties of local cacti, trees, and shrubs. An impressive monument on the capitol grounds pays tribute to World War I hero Frank Luke, Jr.

Phoenix has several interesting museums. The Heard Museum of Anthropology and Primitive Arts is one of the finest of its type. It was built and endowed by Mr. and Mrs. Dwight B. Heard. Relics of Arizona pioneer days are preserved in the Arizona State Museum, and the Phoenix Art Museum is maintained by the Phoenix Fine

Capitol Complex in Phoenix.

Grady Gammage Memorial Auditorium.

Arts Association. The American Heritage Wax Museum in Scottsdale is an especially fine example of its type. Music lovers may hear the Phoenix Symphony and most of the great artists on tour.

On the campus of Arizona State University at Tempe is one of the country's most unusual buildings, the circular Grady Gammage Memorial Auditorium, designed by Frank Lloyd Wright. Seating three thousand persons, its most distant seat is only 115 feet (35 meters) from the stage. The balconies are detached from the rear wall so that sound travels completely around and through the building. The 145-foot (44-meter) box girder supporting the grand tier is probably the largest of its kind ever used.

Another Frank Lloyd Wright enterprise is his home-office-architectural school, Taliesin West, twenty-six miles (forty-two kilometers) northeast of Phoenix.

The city of Phoenix now owns its ancient predecessor metropolis, prehistoric Pueblo Grande. When poor drainage and floods forced the inhabitants to abandon Pueblo Grande, they left the aged and sick to take care of themselves as best they could while the young and strong went on to better surroundings.

The Desert Botanical Garden in Papago Park claims to be the best of its kind in the world. The park also houses Phoenix's outstanding zoo. Arizona's first and long-time governor, George W.P. Hunt, is buried in Papago Park, his grave marked by a white pyramid.

Through its Don's Club, Phoenix is served by one of the most unusual and energetic of all civic booster groups. The members strive to keep alive the lore and tradition of the region. One of their most famous enterprises is the annual Superstition Mountain Lost Gold Trek. This is a mock search for the legendary Lost Dutchman Mine, an all-day hike and exploration enhanced by tales of Western lore, entertainment, and food. The trek has become so popular that all reservations are taken weeks in advance.

NORTHERN ARIZONA

Flagstaff is the unofficial capital of the vast reaches of northern Arizona. To celebrate the nation's centennial in 1876, a group of travelers trimmed a tall pine into a flagstaff and raised an American flag. A settlement grew up around the trimmed tree. The flagstaff remained a landmark for many years and eventually gave the city its name. The county seat of Coconino County—second largest in area in the country—Flagstaff is known as an intellectual center, with Northern Arizona University, nearby Museum of Northern Arizona, and Lowell Observatory adding to this reputation.

For one of the largest annual festivals in western America, more than ten thousand Indians come to Flagstaff from all over the West for the All-Indian Powwow. Visitors are fascinated by the tent encampment at the powwow grounds. One of the best exhibits of Indian art is the Hopi Craftsman Show held at the same time as the powwow.

Coconino County contains four national monuments: the massive cinder cone of Sunset Crater, remains of twelfth-century Wupatki National Monument, 400-foot (122-meter) deep Walnut Canyon, with ruins of three hundred small prehistoric cliff dwellings, many of them tiny caves carved in the cliff, and, of course, the Grand Canyon.

Some of the world's most spectacular scenery is found in less well-known Oak Creek Canyon. Some say the experience of driving through this wonderland of rocks and color is equal to that of the Grand Canyon.

Montezuma Castle National Monument and Tuzigoot National

Monument rank high among the sites of prehistoric Arizona preserved by the government. Another preserved town is not historic. When the booming mine town of Jerome ran out of ore, it became the country's most recent large ghost town. Its houses perch precariously on the steep slopes, propped up by beams and boulders. Many of the buildings have tumbled down. There is a 1,500-foot (457-meter) difference in elevation from one part of town to another. Those few of its former population of fifteen thousand who remained formed the Jerome Historical Society, and the lively ghost town is now host to large numbers of tourists who want to see its many points of interest. Jerome was named by and for Winston Churchill's distant cousin, Eugene Jerome.

Prescott calls itself the Cowboy Capital of the World. The Smoki Indians, a bogus tribe of Prescott businessmen, preserve Indian customs and perform many Indian rites.

Northeast Arizona comes to a point in the only place in the United States where four states join at their points—a vast region called the Four Corners. In the northeast are many interesting sites of Navajo and Hopi culture: the "Technicolor mirage" of the Painted Desert, the chocolate-colored Grand Falls of the Little Colorado, Petrified Forest National Park, Navajo National Monument, Canyon de Chelly National Monument, and Meteor Crater, where a prehistoric "visitor" from outer space made a hole in the ground. Other interesting places include Walpi Village, perched high on a cliff, a favorite subject of artists; the world's highest steel arch bridge, over Glen Canyon; stupendous Glen Canyon Dam; and Page, Arizona's newest town, at Glen Canyon Dam.

In Monument Valley, shared with Utah, an aura of mystery and sighing silence pervades. Great stone skyscrapers raise their silhouettes against the desert sky. Among the most famous of these many formations is the pair of "mittens," one mitten in Arizona and the other in Utah.

Dominating northeast Arizona is the first of America's huge canyon dams—Hoover—with its wonderful opportunities for sport and pleasure in the enormous Lake Mead National Recreation Area. Another interesting sight is Pipe Spring National Monument.

88

GRANDEST OF THE GRAND

The Grand Canyon cannot be described by writers or captured by artists or photographers in any true sense. Almost every part of this huge area has wonders of its own in brilliant color: strange formations, rocks and fossils, plant or animal life, pueblo ruins, the Havasupai community, waterfalls, magnificent trees clinging to the walls. The overall effect is almost overwhelming.

One of the little-known facts of interest about the canyon is the change in climate and vegetation from bottom to top. On the canyon floor the climate of the Mexican desert prevails. As the gradual ascent is made, the climate changes until on the north rim the climate is that of southern Canada—the whole width of the United States in relation to climate can be traversed in one trip up the canyon wall. In winter the north rim is closed by snows, but the south rim is open all winter to visitors.

Bright Angel Lodge, El Tovar Hotel, and other facilities are available on the south rim. El Tovar has been built of native boulders and pine logs and has a rustic interior to blend with the surroundings. Yavapai Museum helps visitors become acquainted with all the many facets of interest about the canyon. Walking and muleback trips descend to the bottom of the canyon. Visitors are thrilled with the experience of staying overnight at the very bottom of the canyon at Phantom Ranch, and the more rugged can arrange for a visit to the Havasupai lands on the canyon floor.

On the north rim is Grand Canyon Lodge. Trips to the canyon bottom also originate from the north rim. Both north and south offer many points where hiker, horseback rider, or motorist can pause to marvel at the canyon in its many aspects—whether in bright sunlight, threatened by a looming thunderstorm, in the eerie glow of moonlight, tufted with glittering white snow, or shimmering in the intense sun.

As President Theodore Roosevelt said when he visited Grand Canyon in 1903, "Do nothing to mar its grandeur ... keep it for your children, your children's children, and all who come after you as the one great sight which every American should see."

Handy Reference Section

Instant Facts

Became the 48th state—February 14, 1912
Capital—Phoenix, settled 1867
Nickname—The Grand Canyon State
State motto—*Ditat Deus* ("God Enriches")
State tree—Palo verde
State flower—Saguaro blossoms
State song—"Arizona"
Area—113,956 square miles (295,145 square kilometers)
Rank in area—6th
Greatest length (north to south)—392 miles (631 kilometers)
Greatest width (east to west)—338 miles (544 kilometers)
Highest point—12,670 feet (3,862 meters), Humphreys Peak
Lowest point—137 feet (42 meters), near Yuma
Number of counties—14
Population—2,352,000 (1980 projection)
Rank in nation—33rd
Population density—20.6 per square mile (7.9 per square kilometer)
Birthrate—18.4 per 1,000
Physicians per 100,000—164

Principal cities—
Phoenix	581,562	(1970 census)
Tucson	262,933	
Scottsdale	67,823	
Tempe	63,550	
Mesa	62,853	
Glendale	36,228	
Yuma	29,007	

You Have a Date with History

1539—Father Marcos de Niza crosses portion of Arizona
1540—Francisco Vasquez de Coronado explores; Garcia Lopez de Cardenas discovers Grand Canyon; Hernando de Alarcon discovers lower Colorado River
1580—Father Augustin Rodriguez attempts mission work
1600—Franciscans begin mission work
1680—Missions destroyed
1692—Father Eusebio Kino begins work
1752—Tubac becomes first permanent European settlement
1768—Father Francisco Tomas Garcés becomes mission leader
1781—Father Garcés murdered by Yuma Indians

1822—Region comes under Mexican control
1824—First United States trappers enter region
1848—Most of present-day Arizona transferred to United States
1853—Gadsden Purchase extends Arizona limits
1861—Civil War reaches Arizona
1863—Territory of Arizona created
1864—Kit Carson moves Navajo to New Mexico
1869—John Wesley Powell traverses Colorado through Grand Canyon
1881—State first crossed by railroad
1886—Arizona State University founded as Tempe Normal School
1887—James Reavis claims vast Arizona tract
1889—Phoenix becomes capital
1891—University of Arizona holds first classes
1901—Capitol building completed at Phoenix
1911—Theodore Roosevelt Dam dedicated by Teddy Roosevelt
1912—Statehood
1913—Grand Canyon made a national park
1917—Frank Luke, Jr., becomes national hero in World War I
1930—Coolidge Dam dedicated by Calvin Coolidge
1936—Hoover Dam commences operation
1964—Glen Canyon Dam completed
1969—Navajo Community College opens at Many Farms
1975—Greatest population growth rate of any state
1978—Phoenix population projected to pass 700,000

Thinkers, Doers, Fighters

Carson, Kit
Cochise (Chief)
Douglas, Lewis W.
Douglas, A.E.
Garcés, Francisco Tomas
Geronimo (Chief)
Goldwater, Barry
Hall, Dick Wick
Hayden, Carl
Hunt, George W.P.
Kino, Eusebio Francisco

Klah, Hosteen
La Farge, Oliver
Lowell, Percival
Luke, Frank, Jr.
Poston, Charles D.
Santee, Ross
Tombaugh, Clyde W.
Wickenburg, Henry
Wister, Owen
Wright, Frank Lloyd
Wright, Harold Bell

Governors of the State of Arizona

George W.P. Hunt 1912-1917
Thomas E. Campbell 1917
George W.P. Hunt 1917-1919
Thomas E. Campbell 1919-1923
George W.P. Hunt 1923-1929
John C. Phillips 1929-1931
George W.P. Hunt 1931-1933
Benjamin B. Moeur 1933-1937
Rawleigh C. Stanford 1937-1939
Robert T. Jones 1939-1941

Sidney P. Osborn 1941-1948
Dan E. Garvey 1948-1951
J. Howard Pyle 1951-1955
Ernest W. McFarland 1955-1959
Paul Fannin 1959-1965
Samuel P. Goddard, Jr. 1965-1967
John R. Williams 1967-1975
Raul H. Castro 1975-1977
Wesley Bolin 1977-1978
Bruce E. Babbitt 1978-

Index

94

PICTURE CREDITS

Color photographs courtesy of the following: Arizona Office of Tourism, 8, 11, 12, 14, 22, 23, 33, 38, 49, 50, 60, 65, 72, 76, 78, 83, 85; USDI, NPS, Navajo National Monument, Cover; USDI, NPS, Wapatki-Sunset Crater National Monuments, 24; USDI, NPS, Tumacacori National Monument, 28, 41, 69; USDI, NPS, Fish and Wildlife Service, 58; Wyoming Travel Commission, 58; USDI, Geographical Survey, 2-3 (map); EROS Data Center, 4-5.

Illustrations on back cover by Len W. Meents.

ABOUT THE AUTHOR

With the publication of his first book for school use when he was twenty, **Allan Carpenter** began a career as an author that has spanned more than 135 books. After teaching in the public schools of Des Moines, Mr. Carpenter began his career as an educational publisher at the age of twenty-one when he founded the magazine *Teachers Digest.* In the field of educational periodicals, he was responsible for many innovations. During his many years in publishing, he has perfected a highly organized approach to handling large volumes of factual material: after extensive traveling and having collected all possible materials, he systematically reviews and organizes everything. From his apartment high in Chicago's John Hancock Building, Allan recalls, "My collection and assimilation of materials on the states and countries began before the publication of my first book." Allan is the founder of Carpenter Publishing House and of Infordata International, Inc., publishers of *Issues in Education* and *Index to U.S. Government Periodicals.* When he is not writing or traveling, his principal avocation is music. He has been the principal bassist of many symphonies, and he managed the country's leading non-professional symphony for twenty-five years.